Poetry and the Body

JOHN VERNON

Poetry and the Body

UNIVERSITY OF ILLINOIS PRESS

Urbana · Chicago · London

Library of Congress Cataloging in Publication Data

Vernon, John, 1943–
  Poetry and the body.

  Bibliography: p.
  Includes index.
  1. Poetics. I. Title.
PN1042.V47   808.1   78-11552
ISBN 0-252-00699-2

FOR ANN

Contents

Introduction

THIS BOOK IS a long essay, divided in parts. In it, I explore the notion that a poem is not an object, but an intersection of subject and object, as the human body itself is. I think this applies to most works of literature and art; we can see it most easily in dance. In fact, the metaphor of dance is one of the central ones in this book. A poet speaks from his body and drives the gestures of his body into the words of his poem, so that the words themselves gesture and dance. Of course, I don't mean to imply that the words on a page rise up and do pirouettes. The words on a page are merely a score; the actual poem consists of words activated, at least in the imagination of the reader, by human speech. "Were you thinking that those were the words, those upright lines? those curves, angles, dots," Whitman asks. "No, the real words are more delicious than they. / Human bodies are words, myriads of words." This is a startling notion, but one not unique to Whitman. Collingwood must have something similar in mind when he says, "Dance is the mother of language," as must Stevens when he says in "Poetry Is a Destructive Force":

> It is a thing to have,
> A lion, an ox in his breast,
> To feel it breathing there.

In other words, a word or a collection of words is first of all an act of the body, a marriage of flesh and air. I know this act couldn't exist without that structure we call language, which is previous to our individual bodies; but on the other hand, language couldn't exist without our bodies to manifest it. And our bodies always manifest it with those qualities we call style, grace, tone, and so forth, qualities which theorists of language seldom talk about, but which are always the first edge of a poem. When I say that words in a poem—or in a good poem—dance, I mean that they have such qualities, and that, in addition, the experience of language in the poem is a kinetic one. Of course, the experience of all language is kinetic, at least in the sense that language is successive and exists in time. In poetry, this kinesis is augmented by any number of devices—repetition, enjambment, the use of periodic sentences—and by the resistance of form, which acts as a kind of current against which the language of a poem must struggle. So, we could say that reading poetry is like rowing upstream against the current, whereas reading prose is like rowing with the current. In the case of prose, the movement may be swift, in the sense that we get where we are going more quickly; but it is also without modulation, purely horizontal. In the case of poetry, the movement is both horizontal and vertical, and it is a movement we are always conscious of as movement. This is equally true of formal and free verse. I think, by the way, that this distinction between poetry and prose is similar to Valéry's statement that prose is like walking, but poetry is like dancing.

My aim in this book is to explore ways of talking about poems that will respect and deal with this kind of bodily movement. So, most of the discussions of poetry and poems are not thematic but formal. But by "form," I don't mean a skin detachable from a poem, or a mold into which the content is poured. Rather, I mean the body of the poem itself, which is at the intersection where what we normally call form and content meet. Another way of putting this is that I want to explore ways of dealing with poems not only as things but as acts, acts whose gestures and whose successive growth and accumulation are as integral to them as the flow of a river is to the river. A poem is not simply a thing, an object. It is subject and object, act and thing, energy and matter. I don't want to show how poems work, but to show them working, to show the process of them working, and to show that this is a physical, visceral process.

The first part of this book deals with language and speech in order to lay the foundation for regarding poems as acts of the body. I should mention that this distinction between language and speech is a standard one among French and German thinkers. As far as I know, I am the first to apply it in an extended manner to poetry, and to an understanding in particular of modern culture and modern poetry. The second part deals specifically with the activity of poetry, and the third part deals with particular poems by Donne, Blake, and Mallarmé. In the case of Donne and Blake, I've chosen to discuss classic and well-known poems, Donne's "Batter My Heart" sonnet and Blake's "The Tyger," in order to search in them for the fresh gestures that made them classics in the first place, before, so to speak, the dust got on them. The fourth part deals with the tradition of modern and contemporary poetry that begins with Whitman and undergoes an important shift in William Carlos Williams and Robert Creeley. This is the tradition of free verse, or "naked poetry," in which the unmediated gesture of speech becomes the heart of the poem. With Williams and Creeley, this gesture becomes increasingly less representational and more a pure act, a dance of words, a mouth.

Readers of contemporary French criticism will note that my premises are the opposite of those of the French. I refer to the French often because I have learned from them, but in a way that one learns from an X-ray, from the negative of oneself. Derrida, for example, believes in the primacy of writing over speech and rejects the notion of an author, what Americans would call the voice or vision or person in or behind the work. The differences between this point of view and my own are actually buried deep in the history of modern literature—in Mallarmé and Whitman, who were so much the opposite of each other we have to remind ourselves they were actually contemporaries. In the chapter on Mallarmé and the section titled "Naked Poetry," I explore these differences. Obviously, one can't understand modern literature without acknowledging that for many writers, following Mallarmé, the act of writing has become primary—has in a sense dissolved the subject—and language has become an end in itself. But this is only one current in modern literature. The tradition that has come down to us from Blake and Whitman is a very different current, and is stronger than ever today. My belief in the primacy of speech over writing, in the importance of language as a bodily act, is not a nostalgia for lost origins, as Derrida or his followers would put it, but rather a reflection of my own experience as a poet and of my love for those contemporary poets who have been nurtured by the tradition of Whitman.

Still, the French have taught us a great deal. We have come to understand that language is a structure as well as an activity, and that even in a poet like Whitman there is a degree to which the language is opaque and autonomous. But the French have a great deal to learn from us as well; we can show them that even Mallarmé has a body, that even the most pure act of writing has a residue of speech, of bodily drama. In fact, the relationship between speech and writing is an extremely complex one, and a danger lies in oversimplifying it with labels. To assert the primacy of speech is not to minimize the importance of writing, or even to bracket it, as many of the French seem to bracket the human body. "I am no doubt not the only one who writes in order to have no face," Michel Foucault says. But my view is that one can't write without a face, that is, without an attitude, an appearance, a style, a way of facing things, all of which Foucault, for one, unmistakably possesses; in other words, one can't write without being embodied.

A great deal of American criticism today seems to be caught between the death of New Criticism and an ambivalent relationship to French thought. The ambivalence is reflected most deeply in the language of criticism. French playfulness becomes American self-indulgence, largely because in America we've found ourselves suddenly released from the requirements of formal analysis and close reading; and the almost sensual relationship to ideas the French are capable of becomes in America bloodless, abstract, jargon-ridden. It seems to me that the alternative is for critics to trust their own language, as the best critics have always done. In America, this means the language that Whitman described as "limber and full enough," the language rooted in our own speech and in our bodies.

A few words about other writers who have dealt with topics at least loosely related to poetry and the body: R. P. Blackmur's "Language as Gesture," while a brief essay, is in a sense the springboard for the first two parts of this book. Blackmur, an American, and Maurice Merleau-Ponty, a Frenchman, both emphasize the bodily, gestural quality of language. Martin Heidegger also, in his later work, talks about language as an activity—a way, a going forth—rather than as an object. These three thinkers are the most important fathers of this book; my goal has been in many respects to elaborate on hints and possibilities contained in their meditations on language.

Several other books have a more peripheral but still significant relationship to this one. Geoffrey Hartman's *The Unmediated
Vision*, particularly in the chapter on Rilke, acknowledges the
importance of voice and body in modern poetry. Francis Berry's
Poetry and the Physical Voice discusses the ways poetry and
certain poets literally sound, in terms of pitch, volume, timbre,
intonation, etc. Stanley Burnshaw's *The Seamless Web* deals
with the general sense of the organic in all the arts and sees the
body as the central figure in a continuous web that weaves all
things together. Berry and Burnshaw each deal with the body
almost exclusively as a biological entity; each makes use of
research in the sciences, particularly in physiology and biology.
A book whose approach is more metaphoric, and therefore
closer to this one, is Cary Nelson's *The Incarnate Word*. Nelson's
intention is to capture at least virtually in the act of criticism the
experience of reading, which, he says, is an experience of folding the text into "the body's house." His emphasis, however, is
on verbal space; mine is on verbal activity, the poem not as a
field—or not only as a field—but as energy, desire, act.

In Part III, my readings of poems are an attempt to reconsti-
tute the experience of the poem as act. I recognize the fact that
there is no such a thing as a naïve reading, a first reading: we
are almost always predisposed in one way or another to a poem
before we come to it. But as Cary Nelson points out, we do
make ourselves provisionally naïve in order to submit to the
experience of the text. My models in this section are two thinkers: Hugh Kenner, in the "Syntax in Rutherford" chapter of
The Pound Era, and the later Heidegger. In discussing a poem,
both Heidegger and Kenner circle away from and back to it,
quoting a bit more each time, until the completed poem
achieves itself. This method not only creates a striking fiction of
the act of reading, but emphasizes the provisional, contingent
sense of the poem, the poem as an act of discovery. Of course,

criticism and reading are not exactly the same; but can we afford to keep them entirely distinct from each other? Any criticism that ignores the experience of a text, the experience of reading, is doomed to create a fiction too, but one that it naïvely regards as "objectivity." The alternative, incidentally, is not impressionism or subjectivity. Criticism that respects the act of reading must respect the text, must *submit* to it. At its best, this kind of criticism releases the poem, allows it to come into its own being.

I should mention one more work whose subject matter bears a relationship to this one: Roland Barthes's *The Pleasure of the Text* (*Le Plaisir du Texte*). Barthes's book is brief, elliptical, fragmented, compressed, often short-circuited, usually brilliant, and almost totally devoid of examples. Much of what he says is true: the text has a human form, is a figure, an anagram of the body; the art of what he calls writing aloud is the art of guiding one's body. These are important notions, but unfortunately they take the form of aphorisms, and we never learn how they operate in actual texts. The best aspect of Barthes's book is the obvious pleasure he takes in his own language, a pleasure that approaches what he calls bliss (*jouissance*) in the final pages. His "language lined with flesh," mentioned on the last page, is in fact the topic of this book. Such a language is, simply: poetry.

I hope it's obvious that this book is not about the theme of the body or the image of the body in poetry, at least not in a literal sense, in the sense that a critic discusses bird imagery in Shakespeare. A book about body imagery in poetry would be volumes long, and I don't envy anyone who would want to write it. This book is rather about the activity of the body in poetry, and about my notion that a poem is not merely an object because the body is not merely an object. My body is the intersection, the fusion, of matter and energy. It is not an object in the sense of being inert, raw material; it is capable of gesturing and leaping out of itself. This is the connection between poetry and the body; the same thing is true of poems. This connection is a fertile and mysterious one, has been largely unexplored by criticism, and is the subject of this book.[1]

[1] Unless otherwise indicated, all translations of poems are by me. I would like to thank Regis Durand of the Université de Lille, Lille, France, for his criticism and assistance in the discussion of Mallarmé's sonnet, as well as for his help in translating it. I would also like to thank the Research Foundation of the State University of New York for a summer grant that enabled me to complete part of this book.

PART I

Language and Speech

ONE Language and the Body

My own sense of the human body is contained in a passage in Rilke's second Duino Elegy:

> Didn't the caution of human gestures on Attic steles
> Amaze you? Weren't love and separation placed
> on those shoulders so lightly they seemed made
> of other stuff than we are? Remember the hands:
> despite the power in the torso, they lie weightless.
> The self-controlled knew this: we can only go so far.
> All we can do is touch one another like this. The gods
> can press down on us much more, but that's the gods' affair.
>
> [trans. A. Poulin, Jr.]

My understanding of this passage is as follows: love has limits, but those limits increase both its power and its expressiveness. The same is true of the human body. A good example to show this is our use of gesture. Gesture is that expressive power of the body by which we simultaneously break through the boundaries of our skin and learn the limits that exist outside us. When we touch, Rilke says, what we hold back will express as much as what we give. But this is only possible if we are completely coextensive with our bodies, rather than simply possess them as objects. If my body were simply flesh and no more, it would be a corpse, so much dead weight. Of course, it *is* flesh; it is a solid, physical reality, with bones, sinews, veins, a heart, intestines, fat, and skin. But it is also, as Norman O. Brown says, "an energy system . . . in perpetual inner self-construction and self-destruction." It is "not a thing or substance, but a continuous creation." I would amend that to say: it is a thing or substance, *and* a continuous creation. The paradox of the body is that it is meat, and it is something that leaps, gestures, speaks, touches. It is a substance, a thing in itself, and it is a means to an end. In the passage from Rilke, there are two bodies: that of the speaker or listener, and that of the figures on Greek steles, which seem "made of other stuff than we are." These two bodies are polarities of everyone's bodily experience. At times, we are oppressively aware of the stuff we are made of, because it weighs our lives down, like Delmore Schwartz's "heavy bear." "Hang the meat on the hook," Charles Simic says, "So that I may see what I am." At other times, our bodies are as loose and liquid as water, and are completely swallowed into our actions, into walking, running, making love, speaking.

This dual nature of the body is not an absolute split; our two bodies slip into and out of each other in their common skin. At its best moments, my body unites matter and energy, like Blake's tyger, perpetually present and perpetually born. Also, at its best moments, my body is not simply my body to the exclusion of all other beings. "All we can do is touch each other like this," Rilke says. Our bodies are doors, sometimes closed and sometimes open, and when they are open they are the means by which we go out into the world and encounter other beings.

Actually, our bodies can't ever be completely closed. If we cut our bodies off from air, food, water, etc., they will die—or, *we* will die. The body is not only an energy system, but a particular kind of energy system continually in touch with the world of things around it. My body is always engaged in acts of transformations, acts caught in a net that well up out of the environ-energy and tissue (and waste). My body *is* these series of transformations, acts caught in a net that well up out of the environment around me.

So my body isn't the only body that exists, and at the same time it is closely woven into the material world around it. That's my starting point for thinking about language. The first thing that strikes me about language is that it's reciprocal. I mean this in two ways: first, I speak to and listen to other people, and second, my speech handles and encounters the resistance of things in the world, the resistance of matter and earth. Language may actually be one of those things "made of other stuff than we are," but it also is involved with my body and so with matter. On the other hand, language may very well be that aspect of material things by which they make themselves available to human grace: a way in which things transcend themselves. I think that this is the point Rilke makes in the Ninth Elegy, when he talks about things transcending themselves through the agency of our words:

> Maybe we're here only to say: *house,*
> *bridge, well, gate, jug, olive tree, window*—
> at most, *pillar, tower* . . . but to say them, remember,
> oh, to say them in a way that the things themselves
> never dreamed of existing so intensely.

> [trans. A. Poulin, Jr.]

Later on in the same Elegy, Rilke says that perishable things become imperishable through our use of language. Of course, he's talking about a particular use of language, poetry. But I think he also means his assertion to apply to all language, to words in general, and to the mysterious connections between the sounds we make with our mouths and the trees, chairs, cats, and stones around us.

So I begin with two points about language: first, it is a bodily activity, and second, it is a transcendent activity, a way our bodies transcend themselves and a way things transcend themselves for us. I think that both of these statements are true, and one couldn't be true without the other. When our bodies participate in language, they participate in an organization that transcends our individual bodies or the individual things around us, an organization with its own rules and patterns and its own history previous to ours. At the same time, the gravity and thingness of the body and earth prevent language from ever flying off and becoming a self-enclosed or self-referring structure, a pure form. This gravity exists *in* language, at its very heart, in our bodily gestures. I would like now to take up these points one at a time in some detail; first, language as an organization, and second, language as a bodily activity.

Language as an organization:

I trust my own experience of language enough to suspect that the way I acquired it is at least analogous to the way the first human beings acquired it. My sense of language acquisition is quite simple: I woke up immersed in language. In other words, to wake up—that is, to have consciousness—and to have language, are synonymous. Who can remember when he first used language? Everything stems from that moment—and it is a moment, not a gradual accretion of moments—but the moment itself is no beginning point. I wake up and find myself swimming in a medium given to me. It's like waking up immersed in a pool of water: I have to keep myself afloat with the actions of my body. I speak because I am immersed in speech; my gestures are a form of treading water.

So I wake up with language, in a world of things with names.

I don't think the things existed before I had language, at least not in the way they do now. That's because I didn't exist before I had language; that is, the "I" didn't exist, the self, consciousness, my little pocket of identity'. First of all, things didn't exist before there were words because thing and word come into existence simultaneously. This doesn't mean that they are identical, but that the organization that enables them to exist, that indicates where they begin and stop, is one and the same for both. By "organization" I mean the setting of things beside each other, the delimiting of things, the drawing of their boundaries. Language in fact *is* that organization. Second, the "I" comes into existence with language, because by virtue of organizing the world we have extricated ourselves from it. Ernst Cassirer says this in *The Philosophy of Symbolic Forms*. When language is born, the "I" and the "world" become separated from each other and establish themselves independently. This word "independently" is actually an oversimplification, in more ways than one. Language doesn't simply construct a homogeneous mass called the "world" and oppose it to the "I." Rather, it distinguishes layers of that world, various distances, classes of objects, separations, categories. It injects corridors into the world, and enables us to walk through them and experience shifting relationships to the objects we encounter. It arranges things in foregrounds and backgrounds, in the past, present, and future, in the singular and plural, in types, colors, sizes, degrees of importance, and so forth.

One of the great insights of modern French thought has been to emphasize this sense of language as an organization or structure. Unfortunately, the assumption now seems to be that that structure is autonomous. Following de Saussure, most French structuralists and post-structuralists assume that language is diacritical and that words derive their meanings not from their referents, but from their relative relationships to each other.

Not only does language "organize reality," it also gives us the word "reality." To look for origins or causes of language is futile; language is circular, words refer to other words.

Of course, there is a great deal of truth to this. Thinking about my own experience, I know that when I use words, the forms of language determine what I will say as much as my feelings, thoughts, or external events or objects do. This is now a truism among French thinkers: language speaks us as much as we speak it. But I prefer to look at if from another point of view. The reason words often (not always) tend to refer to other words is that the things they are supposed to refer to are continually eluding their grasp. I think there's usually a tug of war going on between words and things. Every day, something is being embalmed by words and something else is escaping them. This is one of the chief paradoxes of language: at the same time that language organizes the world, the world resists language. I'll emphasize that: *language organizes the world—the world resists language*. Poets often feel this—feel things themselves resisting what they say. That's because poets aren't interested in categories, classes, types, sizes, degrees of importance, singular and plural, so much as they are in the thing in front of them, the thing itself. Poets also know that there is a lot that is unnameable in the thing itself. All this unnameability of things tends to collect together, and then we give it a general name: "reality" or "world." The world is that very unnameable thing that resists language; it is what language organizes, but that very organization gives rise to its resistance, enables it to resist. In other words, the world resists language where *this* tree, *this* stone, *this* chair have no names. Language sifts everything through its categories and types, and the world is the deposit left over when language has finished. Language impregnates the world, and the world sheds language.

I'm conscious of this strange relationship between language

and the world as I write these words. I can write anything I want to. Noam Chomsky's famous example is "colorless green ideas sleep furiously." Language has no obligation to "reality"; reality is the lie that makes language true. Yet, where would what we call "the world" or "reality" be without a language that breaks it down into manageable pieces for us? Without language, it would be a homogenous swap, lacking even a foreground and background.

I think what I'm trying to describe is the curious way in which the world of my experience, which has already been impregnated, shaped, and organized by language, is at the same time strangely untouched by it, or is always disappearing into the interstices between words. I've already said there are no things previous to words; yet, at the same time, *everything* is previous to words. Just when we think we have it all organized, one orange peel slips out of place, or a bird becomes extinct and passes completely into language, and then the whole structure shifts and leans to one side and spills out of itself. The clearest way I can formulate this—or the most convenient way for now—is to say that the relationship between language and the world is one of continual unrest, resistance, tension. *Language organizes the world—the world resists language.* My evidence for this tension is the human body and the gestures we make. That brings me to the second point

Language as a bodily activity:

If I were speaking this to you instead of writing it, I would probably be gesturing as I speak. By "gestures" I mean not only arm movements and facial expressions, but all the physical vehicles of nuance and expression that accompany speech— pitch, tone, loudness, quickness, pause, repetition, etc. But I mean especially arm and hand movements, facial expressions, and body movements: the ways we orchestrate speech. Gestures are a kind of penumbra surrounding my words, an inchoate jumble of bodily motions flocking around my words like pigeons around pieces of bread. Often, they increase their activity when a lot of verbs are present in speech; they describe not so much the actions the verbs designate, but the inner contours of those actions: whether they begin suddenly or gradually, come to a conclusion or are incomplete, are uneven or continuous, and so forth. I think of gestures as impulses that well up from inside me, and move outward, only to be caught in the net or web of my body, which distributes them across its surface, sluggishly across the torso, but more and more quickly and delicately along the upper extremities—the shoulders, arms, face, hands, fingers—as if the original impulse were a kind of whip that hardly moves at its base, but that sweeps out and cracks at its tip.

Gestures exist for the most part below the brink of choice; they are involuntary activities. Maybe that's why they have such an ambiguous relationship to meaning; some of them are purely expressive, and some are representational in a much more immediate way than even language is. That is, the gesture with meaning doesn't just clothe the meaning, but rather is its body, its existence. If I raise my open hand to my brow and rub it slowly, this not only represents weariness, this *is* weariness. The language of gestures is the closest thing we have to the natural or pure language that romantic philosophers like Novalis searched for: a language in which the relationship between the sign and what it signifies is not arbitrary, but necessary, so that sign and meaning are one. Speech, in fact, begins as gesture, as an expressive play of sounds the mouth makes. Most of our gestures, however, don't want to mean, or, to put it another way, are purely expressive without expressing any particular thing. This is because most gestures accompany speech, which *does* want to mean, and which carries enough of a burden of meaning to allow our gestures free play around its edges. Actually, the difference between speech and gestures isn't one of kind but of degree. They are both equally bodily activities; but one has accumulated more meaning than the other, by attaching itself to (or evolving from within itself) that transcendent structure we call language. This is the important point to make for now: the organization called language is always and only manifest in our bodies and in our bodily activities. Even during the most lofty flights of speech, the body and the gestures of the body, the thickness of the tongue and lips that give weight to the breath of language, and the fleshiness of the arms that gesture to keep the body afloat in language—all these serve as an anchor to language. If language organizes the world, and the world resists language—if there is a tension between the world and language—the human body is this tension itself, and gestures are its visible vibration, the graph of its oscillations. Gestures are the key to the relationship between language and the world.

Think of it this way: gestures may very well be leftovers of all the grasping and releasing we do as infants. First we grasp and release things, then we make the same gestures in the air when we want something. Then we come to designate things, to point them out, with the same gestures. Finally, we come to make a kind of pure act of designation with those same gestures, now barely recognizable. It occurs to me that all gestures, no matter how purely expressive, that is, no matter how lacking in meaning, at least have this one residue of meaning: they designate, point, show, reveal. And to do this, according to Heidegger, is the essence of speech (see *On the Way to Language*). To do this also assumes that there is a world of things that our speech and gestures attempt to deal with. Gestures show that speech has an opening and something to open on to. Speech is always a direction, a flight, a vector; it leans forward, pursues.

Gestures are not simply accidental appendages to speech. Rather, speech *needs* gestures: to open up the stubborn resistance of the world that refuses to be spoken, to free blockages and find paths around those that can't be freed—and finally, when all else fails, to carry the excess tension, the stresses of the body out into the air, like flying buttresses. Like flying buttresses, gestures are a solution that is also graceful and elegant, are added on, that is, extra, because they are essential. They are also a measure of the imperfect structure of language, or rather, of the imperfect intersection of language and the world, an intersection ruptured by jagged edges, holes, alleys, cul-de-sacs. When we gesture we are negotiating this intersection. I think of one of Marcel Marceau's marvellous sketches: a man in darkness feels along walls for a door. The walls proliferate at all angles; Marceau's hands, larger and flatter than hands could ever be in air, call them into existence desperately, a labyrinth of endless walls.

Just so with our gestures: we feel along the edges of the world, at that boundary where the world is about to disappear into meaning. Through gestures, our speech incorporates the silent, unspoken presence of the world, but in such a way that it remains silent, unspoken. The world isn't translated by or represented by speech, but rather is a kind of unperceived mountain existing in the midst of speech. Gestures make this existing possible, expressing or signaling it, describing its outline, respecting its region. Gestures are a kind of waterfall always moving forward, because they are an overflow, an excess of speech, and because they describe a presence that dwells within speech, a cliff continually welling up and advancing with the advance of speech. This cliff is the world of things.

I'm trying to express with these metaphors the complex, mysterious relationship between language and the world. We don't "see" the world in language in the same way we see a landscape in a window. The world doesn't appear in language so much as disappear into it. At the same time, language disappears into the world, in the sense that the organization the world has for us *is* language. So the world and language are each, in relation to the other, both transparent and opaque; in fact, they overlap, and each has a residue the other can't touch. And the intersection between them is a sliding, shifting one. Gestures show us that the theater for this intersection, this tug and pull, is the human body. The body introduces language into the world in the form of speech; and the body introduces the world into language in the form of matter, weight, flesh thrust up inside speech.

TWO Language and Speech

AGAIN, IF I WERE speaking this to you instead of writing it, I would be gesturing. In some languages, speaking and gesturing are inseparable. The Zuni Indians, for example, have certain words that must be accompanied by hand gestures in order to be comprehensible. As Cassirer says, "the hands are so closely bound up with the intellect that they seem to form a part of it." But in most languages, speech eventually breaks off from the web of gestures and sign languages and establishes itself separately. Sounds are capable of greater articulation, greater speed and variety, more gradations of stress, rhythm, pace, and volume, more subtle degrees of tone, than gestures. Still, sounds can never match the immediacy—and truthfulness—of facial gestures, for example. Words can create thickets, clouds; anger can find excuses in them, or be dispersed by them—or, conversely, be created by them. Fortunately, a face is closer to the seat of emotions than words; a face can often betray words. This happens often to politicians, teachers, and even actors. One of the wonderful things about speech is that its seat is in the face and that facial gestures accompany words. Speech may break off from the web of gestures, in the sense of refining and sharpening itself, but it never leaves those gestures behind. It may even be that gestures, facial gestures especially, become capable of expressing more once speech discovers that there is more to express. This power of speech to feed its energy back into gestures only serves to show how physical an act speech itself is. Speech is more focused and exact than gestures, but it is just as much an act of the body. Widsith released his word-hoard not as if they were mere sounds but as if they were an army.

In fact, speech is a kind of physical possession, almost as if there were a demon inside me. There is a demon: my body. I never know what my body is revealing or hiding in my act of speaking. If I were standing in front of you, speaking and gesturing, I could be revealing more of myself than I'd care to. I mean this not only to refer to gestures that reveal my bodily style or attitude, but also to pauses, stutters, hesitations, slips of the tongue, mispronunciations—and, within the realm of words themselves, to euphemisms, retractions, false starts, to words skulking away from a fact, to missing words, contradictions, righteous ejaculations, apologies. I think I am choosing, selecting my words; but words just as often choose me. Actually, the act of speaking is seldom a process of selecting. I release what is already there, the words that build up a certain pressure against my tongue. This pressure is not something held back; it's always on the edge of speech, and its effects are evident only in retrospect, when speech has *been* released. I love the floating spontaneity of speech, but I find it disquieting to realize that speech is something speaking within me, an almost autonomous activity that builds up against my tongue. Words seem to call each other up as if they were already attached, and speech seems to have a will of its own. This has a lot to do with the fact that speech is not given to us as a completely empty field to roam in, but comes in the form of conditions and rules, in the form of thought and feeling already to some degree channeled. That is, speech comes in the form of language. When I speak it's as if I'm wading in language, in a series of currents that carry certain words, rhythms, phrases, structures, images, and sounds, unexpectedly past me, from buried or hidden sources.

In fact, this is my definition of speech. Speech is a wading through language, a wading that occurs inside as well as outside the body. Furthermore, that aspect of speech by which it has a will of its own, that aspect of words by which they choose us, is language itself. The amazing thing is that we are never conscious of this will being in conflict with our own. A certain current picks us up, and we find we have chosen that direction. But it's more complicated than that. We can work our way over to eddies and currents—we can swim—and we can alter the force, the speed, the direction of our course. But we are helpless caught in a great swell, a tidal wave, a torrent of words. Yet we know that this torrent is of our own making too. That is, it is and it isn't of our own making. We didn't make language; in some ways it made us. But we each channel it in a certain way, we each speak it with a certain style. Language enables us to speak, while at the same time we enable language to speak.

This relationship between language and speech is a complicated and confusing one, and perhaps the best way to deal with it is to schematize it, even at the risk of oversimplification. In the first place, language is what speech speaks; but speech is what *we* speak. Speech is a flight, a desire, a movement. Language is static and indifferent, a medium whose resistance we have to produce ourselves by wading in it, that is, by speaking. Language is a collection of relationships, a structure; it doesn't have style, expression, or a body; it has to borrow these from us when we wade through it. Speech is suffused with style and

expression because it is imbedded in gestures. Imagine a tele-
scope in which speech emerges from gestures and language
emerges from speech. At first, there are only gestures, a kind of
dumb, inarticulate speech, a thickness and fumbling of the
tongue transferred to the arms and hands—a speech without
words, a speech without language. Gestures are a kind of wallowing below language, or a groping toward language; in one
sense, they never achieve language, but in another, they do: in
speech. Speech is the one thing that gestures and language have
in common. Speech is, at the same time, the heart of a gesture
and the body of language. Gestures and language exist at the
opposite ends of a spectrum, but speech is spread out across the
entire spectrum.

I would like to look at this spectrum more closely. We could
say, in a sense, that there are two orders of human expression,
existing at either end of this spectrum. At one end, there are
gestures, faces, and a whole host of other activities that "speak"
in the same kind of silent way; symbols, dreams, paintings,
music, dance, even posture and behavior. These are all a kind of
inarticulate language, transparent but dumb, all a speech without language. At the other end is language itself, and at the
furthest extreme of language, numbers and mathematical signs.
Numbers are in a sense names deprived of anything to name,
names with all traces of energy, urgency, expression scraped
out of them. They are empty names, language cut off from the
world. If we can accept the picture of this spectrum, some of the
important differences between gestures, speech, and language
become clear. With the first order of expression—gestures,
faces, dreams, etc.—the signified and signifier (or sign) are
indistinguishable. We can't separate a face from what it expresses. This is true whether the expression is "natural" or
"conventional." An example of natural expression is staring
into space, which expresses vacancy; an example of conven-

tional expression is wrinkling the brow, which expresses puzzlement. The latter had to acquire its meaning but is just as immediately and unambiguously expressive as the former. The second order is unambiguous too, but not in an expressive way. Numbers—and words as they approach the condition of numbers, technical words, scientific words, bureaucratic words—are absolutely sealed off from each other. You can't mistake one number for another. This is because they are defined by their positions in relation to each other, that is, by being part of a grid, an abstract system. The first order is so immersed in the particular that it could never fit into an abstract system. There is this face, that painting, this gesture, and they have little to say to each other, unless speech intervenes. The second order always tends to create a sequence wider than itself: 1, 2, 3, 4, 5, 6 . . . . The first order can't make a grid or system because it can't be broken down, recorded, or retransmitted. Paintings can be reproduced, but not in such a way as to generate more paintings. A painting disappears into the air just as much as a sonata, because its parts are always swallowed into the whole instead of being elements in a system. Furthermore, paintings are both expressive and communicative, while numbers are exclusively communicative. Still, we're never sure what they communicate; in a sense, they're the empty form of communication. The first order evokes, while the second order *informs*. The second order is capable of endless substitutions: "a" can be substituted for 1, "b" for 2, "c" for 3, etc. But the first order is rich with singularity: a painting, a dream, are driven into themselves—nothing can be substituted for them. The first order is full, in the manner of a body without clothing, and the second order is empty, in the manner of clothing without a body. The second order organizes things that already exist, by ranging them in sequences. The first order organizes things by calling them into existence. For example, a certain posture in the world can bring things into existence—if we stand up, distances, and if we bend over, hiding places. Or music, as Wallace Stevens knew, can give form to the world:

> And when she sang, the sea,
> Whatever self it had, became the self
> That was her song, for she was the maker.

The first order is contingent, the second order necessary. The first, out of its silence, gives birth to speech; the second, at its extremity, is speech's limit.

In between the two, ranging over the spectrum, speech is that activity in which gesture and information come together or are held apart. We can stand back, as it were, from our speech, and allow our words to speak themselves, clearly and dispassionately. Or, we can raise or modulate our voice, and even, in certain situations, allow speech to spill forward into the silence of gestures, into slamming a hand down on the table or reaching forward to touch someone's arm.

THREE Language and Writing

I'VE TALKED a great deal about speaking and gesturing, but all this time I've been sitting at my desk, writing. My writing is an attempt to be a kind of speech, to incorporate the rhythms of speech; still, it's different from actually talking with you. In the first place, there's no response when I write; this is both the power and impotence of writing, something that Rimbaud expressed over a century ago when he said that "I alone have the key to this mad circus!" If I alone have the key, that's a tremendous advantage, a power; and yet, this "I" with the key is consequently isolated, sealed off, imprisoned—as Rimbaud knew.

Because there's no response when I write, because there's no Other, the Other becomes dislocated and lodges partly in me, partly in language itself. A gap opens up both in language and on this side of language. This gap is what we call the subject. Writing makes the subject possible by cutting speech off from a reply, from other people who speak. Normally, when we speak, the "I" disappears into what we say. If, when language is born, the "I" and the world separate from each other, then when writing is born, the "I" becomes a kind of dislocated Other. The Other, the reply, becomes locked in ourselves; "myself is an other," Rimbaud said. Speaking is an act that opens; it leans forward, out of itself—it is a direction, a projection, a going forth. Speaking bristles with gestures, which buoy it up. When we speak we are swimming in language; our gestures help to propel us forward. Some writers are able to incorporate this tendency of speaking into their writing; the Other enters the words as the expectation of a response, and opens the words in the mode of speech. Literally, there never is a response, at least immediately; yet, the best writing is reciprocal, is a mode of address which not only wakens the Other, but in which the Other wakens the words. This happens, for example, in letter writing. A good poem could even be thought of as a letter. Actually, verse letters are a genre in themselves; most of the great poets in English wrote them. Richard Hugo's "Letters to Friends" are the same form existing today.

Still, writing is largely a reflexive act, and it's probably true that the ego as such, the self-conscious "I," didn't exist before writing existed. Writing opens up within itself a pocket, an enclosure, a space separated from the space around us. This is partly because the act of writing is gestureless; my face is impassive, and only one of my arms moves, not in an expressive but functional way. Again, an exception has to be made for poetry, and for that aspect of all writing we call "poetic." In poetry, the literal act of putting pen to paper may be gestureless, but the gestures instead become incorporated in the very words themselves, in the way the words grasp at each other, in the leaping rhythms between the words—in the *dance* of words. The paradox of poetry is that this dance, which is fully a dance, exists in a permanent, frozen state in writing. To make a poem dance, you must read it aloud and restore it completely to speech. But most writing has no need to be restored to speech.

Most writing is "hardened language," as Roland Barthes puts it, in contrast to speech, which disappears in the air. It's as if we're holding a mirror to speech, but a mirror that records and preserves everything we say. Instead of a plastic, bodily means to express puzzlement, disgust, love, or joy, writing often becomes a hardened means that refuses to support any gestures, feelings, impulses, or emotions. So an inner space opens up, a space we call that of the subject; and into that space, herded together in order to exist, come joy, disgust, love, or puzzlement. Here, they don't need a bodily surface or external form; here the subject becomes subjectivity, and dwells completely within itself.

I am telescoping a lot of history together now: when language comes into existence, the "I" and the world separate; when writing comes into existence, the "I" becomes conscious of itself, becomes a subject, an ego; and the "harder" writing becomes—that is, the more language takes on the character of an object, something out there to be manipulated and bent into shape—the more the subject becomes closed off and dwells within itself. The invention of printing is probably the first stage in this hardening of writing, and the mushrooming of magazines, newspapers, and illustrated weeklies in the nineteenth and twentieth centuries is the most recent stage. There's no doubt that subjectivity first surfaces in literature in the nineteenth century. Julien Sorel's story in *The Red and the Black* is the story of an education in subjectivity, of the ability to withhold one's compliance and one's autonomy from the external world. The same is true of de Sade, Baudelaire, Poe, Rimbaud. Rimbaud's "Seven-Year-Old-Poets" (translated by Wallace Fowlie) is a description of the same education:

> All day he sweated obedience; very
> Intelligent; yet dark twitchings, a few traits,
> Seemed to testify in him to bitter hypocrisy.

> In the shadow of the corridors with their moldy hangings,
> Passing through he stuck out his tongue, his two fists
> In his groin, and in his closed eyes saw spots.

This isolation of the subject, its flight into itself, existed for
Rimbaud most fully in writing:

> At seven, he wrote novels about life
> In the great desert, where exiled Freedom shines,
> Forests, suns, riverbanks, plains!—He was helped
> With illustrated newspapers where, blushing, he saw
> Spanish and Italian girls laugh.

These illustrated newspapers were a new and popular phenom-
enon in Rimbaud's time. In the poem, they fire the imagination
of the child by providing a kind of subjective space isolated and
protected from the actual space he lives in. Deserts, forests,
freedom, laughter, blushing all exist in this space, out of which
the child weaves his novels. Meanwhile, the actual space
around him seems to consist of so much grey raw material:
corridors with moldy hangings, closed shutters, outhouses, alleys, dirty sheets. At the end of the poem, the child lies on a
sheet while the noise of the neighborhood goes on outside him,
and he imagines the sheet is a sail, carrying him away. We are
left with an almost absolute split between inner and outer; the
only correspondence between them is hypocrisy, or irony.

The popularity of newspapers, weeklies, illustrated
magazines hasn't abated; newspapers especially are a permanent part of our lives. In addition, advertising, flyers, junk
mail, billboards, and signs have become some of the chief forms
in which we confront language today. Our culture is the first for
which language has become so completely an object. It's no
wonder that writing increasingly seals itself off from a response
and forms a kind of shell or armor around the subject. Language
no longer exists as it does in speech on this side of the mouth,

as a pressure against the tongue, but outside, surrounding me, pressed into paper—as a thing. The "obscurity" and "refusal to communicate" of modern writers at the turn of the century was supposedly a reaction to the pollution of language by mass media. But in fact, both were results of the same cultural shift, by which language was becoming more and more an object. This shift is also reflected in the attitude of scientists and philosophers toward language. Roland Barthes, Michel Foucault, and others have pointed out that whereas in the eighteenth century language was a transparency, a collection of representations that "flowed and left no deposit" (Barthes), in the nineteenth and twentieth centuries language has taken on a substance and weight, an opacity. Philologists and linguists study its laws just as other scientists study the laws of material beings. The authority and prestige of linguistics and language study in universities testifies to this.

But what does it mean for our experience of language to regard it as an object? In the first place, there is a resistance of things to be named. Language has become an entity sufficient unto itself, circular and self-referring, severed from the world of things. When Wittgenstein says "if the words 'language,' 'experience,' 'world,' have a use, it must be as humble a one as that of the words 'table,' 'lamp,' 'door,' " he is expressing this view of language. Names no longer open onto things; they are objects like those things themselves, tags that they wear, or clothes—and things easily slip out of them. "Looking at a pot, for example, or thinking of a pot, at one of Mr. Knott's pots, of one of Mr. Knott's pots, it was in vain that Watt said, Pot, pot. . . .Watt preferred on the whole having to do with things of which he did not know the name, though this too was painful to Watt, to having to do with things of which the known name, the proven name, was not the name, any more, for him" (Beckett, *Watt*). This gap between words and things means that the intimate tension that normally exists between language and the world has been neutralized; so it has to be recovered, reconstituted, created again. Modern poetry is the history of that recreation. Its chief weapon is the fact that it is poetry, that is, speech; its chief obstacle is the fact that speech is continually being eluded by history in this century. Things are continually outstripping words, and words are left behind as lies. In *Lady Chatterley's Lover*, D. H. Lawrence points out that the important words were canceled out for the generation of World War I. The important words were "honor," "courage," "patriotism," etc. But these weren't canceled out; politicians and journalists continued to use them. Many writers used them too, even some poets. But they no longer called forth the things they signified; they were shells, husks, debris of words, fragments, bits and pieces. Eliot's and Pound's use of fragments of language was brilliant; but they were still fragments, still a brittle language without the suppleness that an inner union with things and history would have given them.

When language becomes an object, it becomes fragmented, broken apart. Words become shells of words. Language itself becomes many languages, each with its own incomplete domain. There is a journalistic language, a scientific language, a legal language, a business language, a street language, a literary language, and so forth. In the course of a day, we pass through many of these languages without even noticing the differences. This is because we have become "subjects" and pass through things in isolation. Language has become our shell, the periphery that surrounds us and defines our subjectivity. Being a subject is the opposite of being a body. For one thing, it means that we have language, but not speech. For another thing, it means that there is an inner life and an outer life, but no connection between them. When Gottfried Benn writes, "That is the man of today, / His inwardness is a vacuum" (in Barnstone, ed., *Modern European Poetry*), he is describing this being a subject. Actually, the word "subject" is inadequate to describe what I am saying, since it has come to mean too many things. For everyone who asserts that the modern age or modern literature is characterized by an increased awareness of the subject, increased exploration of the inner recesses of the self, a private search for identity, and so forth, someone else asserts that this same age or literature is characterized by a loss of self, an evaporation of the subject, and increased anonymity and objectivity. In fact, what our age is characterized by is the self-enclosure of the "I," which can result in either fullness or emptiness, but not both. When whole communities and even nations oscillate between atomistic individualism and fascistic unity, they are caught in the revolving door of that self-enclosed "I," by which one can identify with oneself or with everything else, but not both. Because "I" and world are so isolated from each other in this century, speech too often becomes transformed into language, and language takes on the character of a tool, an object we use and discard. Actually, language has no character; language is like a street in Los Angeles, where an English Tudor house stands next to a Spanish hacienda, next to a colonial American, next to a ranch house. Even the several historical languages that Michel Foucault traces in *The Order of Things* have never really drifted into the past, but exist today among the fragments. There is a Renaissance language, opaque and pregnant with significance in poetry. There is a classical language, transparent and functional in realistic fiction, which despite all the experiments in fiction, is more popular than ever today. And there is a literary language that exists for its own sake; Foucault situates it in the pure act of writing, "where it can possess neither sound nor intelocutor, where it has nothing to say but itself, nothing to do but shine in the brightness of its being." But even in literature this is only one mode of writing; in fact, modern literature like modern culture may be characterized not so much by a certain kind of language as by many languages, overlapping languages. At the same time that Mallarmé was engaged in a pure act of writing and inventing modern literature, Melville and Whitman were inventing another kind of modern literature studded with impurities, with writing stolen from Shakespeare, the Bible, religious sermons, journalism, Egyptian poetry in translation. Of course, Melville and Whitman each had his own unique voice, his own way of bringing these together and synthesizing them, or at least of carrying them along on a single current. But was there a single current that carried them both along and included Mallarmé also? The question that strikes us today is not so much whether there is a literary kind of writing that tries to restore language to its being, but whether there is *any* mode of writing capable of bringing all the fragmented languages together and giving them some common meaning.

At first, the answer that occurs to me is no. When "I" and world become as separated as they have today, the world tends to be neglected, to lose the synthesis an "I" could bring to it, and to fall apart into fragments. "One cannot speak of being any more," says Beckett," one must speak only of the mess." This is true of language as well. Modern culture is a mess, a junk-heap, a secondhand store, and language reflects this state. I love the way Wallace Stevens puts it in "The Man on the Dump":

Is it a philosopher's honeymoon, one finds
On the dump? Is it to sit among mattresses of the dead,
Bottles, pots, shoes and grass and murmur *aptest eve:*
Is it to hear the blatter of grackles and say
Invisible priest; is it to eject, to pull
The day to pieces and cry *stanza my stone?*
Where was it one first heard of the truth? The the.

Not only is this culture a mess in terms of words and things continually swirling around us, in terms of the continual bombardment of sense impressions, but also in more general respects. This is an age of subjectivity, and yet our inwardness, as Benn says, is a vacuum. We are both divorced from our bodies and driven too deeply into them. Exploitation and compassion exist side by side, often in the same person, at the same time. This is an age in which all things are possible, but few things seem stable. "Days pass like papers from a press. / The bouquets come here in the papers" (Stevens). At times, the overwhelming particularity of our culture seems to be its only stable feature. This particularity was given to us by the science with which we entered the century. According to that science, the world is constructed of material objects that obey certain natural laws. These objects are discrete and abundant; not abundant in the sense of a nature that overflows herself, but rather in the sense of things that collect, pile up. Of course, there are laws organizing and arranging these things. And if we want to understand those laws and make use of things, we have to be sober and efficient and methodical in our thinking. "One rejects the trash," Stevens says.

But no sooner did our century begin than a ghost appeared and started undermining this sobriety. This ghost was science itself, but science that had discovered its alter ego. The closer science looked at things the more it discovered their quirkiness, their refusal to obey laws or remain inert, their fluidity rather than their solidity. Einstein, Heisenberg, and others discovered that matter is a warp in the time-space continuum, that very small objects—subatomic particles—are indistinguishable from their movement, that light is sometimes a stream of particles in empty space, and sometimes a series of waves in a medium, and that most of the "laws of nature" are based on probability, not certitude. Still, the particularity of things hasn't been discarded. The view that the world is raw material, an abundance of discrete things, is the basis of technology, and for that reason is intimately involved with the economics, the management of labor and time, the very face and texture of the world we've created. But another world, a world of change and uncertainty, has entered like a ghost into that one and emptied it of its privilege, erased its boundaries and edges, washed away its stability. So there is one way at least to make sense of our culture: precisely by this duality. Our world is one which holds out things and withdraws them at the same time, which is haunted by a double in the form of a trickster, so that every time it achieves certainty, this certainty is shown to be only a convenience, and every time it yields up a permanence, the permanence starts to flow and change.

I've strayed from the topic, but the fact is that this double nature of the world we live in has an impact on language. First of all, our culture isn't simply a mess; the mess takes certain forms, has a tendency, a direction. And language, objectified by writing and fragmented by being made an object, is closely bound up with this tendency. In a sense, you could say that language *is* this tendency, since it is nothing other than the way we shape a world, the organization we give it; in other words, it is culture. Today, language has been dissected and analyzed by linguists and exploded by the proliferation of media. Writing drags the "I" in a kind of pouch behind its words, but this "I" is an emptiness, a lack, and writing itself is brittle and flat. I'm not simply talking about literature, but about writing in general—newspapers, magazines, words, opinions, explanations, instructions, memos, reports, forms, accounts. Language is willing to take any form we give it, willing to bend, stretch, distort itself, willing to disguise our feelings, lie for us, sell us things, manipulate us. It is willing to be anything to enable us to be nothing. It has infinite resources, and can fill any silence that frightens us. It is a confidence man, a Proteus, a chameleon, but it is also a series of material designations that obey certain mechanical laws. We can pick up letters and words, give them a vivid color, and place them against a photograph of the mountains or the Eiffel Tower, and so make people think of cigarettes, soap, towels, or hotels.

On the other hand, language is a ghost, a presence, a perpetual other in our midst. It is a mystery. We are only learning now how completely and thoroughly it invades our world, structures it, gives it to us. But it is a wonder we have learned that, because language is something that always fades away beneath itself as soon as we look at it. It fades away and leaves words behind, ink, impressions on a page. And we think these are language.

In the following parts of this book, I want to look at ways in which ink and impressions on a page are not language, but the shells of language, traces where language has been. I want to look at language in poetry not as a static series of designations, but as a presence, a mystery, and as an act, the act of speech. Modern poetry has the objectification of language to struggle against, which makes it both more desperately kinetic on the one hand, and more subject to fragmentation on the other. This is why most modern poems are lyrics: because a lyric is a brief epiphany, a fragment of consciousness, and yet at the same time an act, a dance of words. Modern poets look at newspapers and billboards, and know that language is something other than that. In a poet like Robert Creeley, speech is a dance that is always threatened by a language outstripped by history, a language left behind by events and therefore a lie, a language which actually drags upon speech. The wonderful thing is that the poem always *is* this struggle. In a poem called "The Language," he says,

> Locate *I*
> *love you* some-
> where in

teeth and
eyes, bite
it but

take care not
to hurt, you
want so

much so
little.

I take this as an attempt to bring the shell of language ("I love you") and the flesh together. Whether they come together, however, isn't as important as the struggle itself, which culminates in the realization at the end of the poem that "Speech / is a mouth." In all poetry, speech is a mouth, that is, a pure act, a presence, not just a representation of something, but the thing itself. We can see this most clearly in modern and contemporary poetry; only in this poetry has speech become so desperately an activity, because only in this poetry has language actually become a threat: the threat of fragmentation, debris, objectification. This is the curse on modern poets: that language may actually be their enemy. In a poet like Donne, for example, there is no contradiction between the static form of a sonnet, which is a gift of language, that is, of culture, and the activity of speech that makes the form come alive. Language is fully taken up by speech, not something speech has to fight against. But in modern poetry, language is often a threat, and the poet has to struggle against it; more on this later.

In all poetry, the center and the essence of the poem—the poetry of it—lies in speech. Language is a ghost that visits speech; or, in the form of writing, language is the shadow of speech. But speech is an act I perform, a searching with words that opens my body. When I speak I am wandering, observing, finding a path, surveying things, walking around them, covering ground, making inquiries, getting lost. When I write I am drawing language around me in order to hole myself up; I want to be in a hole, because no one can touch me there. If I am in a hole, and everyone else is in a hole, if we are all "subjects," then we can send each other messages. We can kidnap language, cut it up, splice it—"Shift linguals—cut word lines," William S. Burroughs says. But if I speak, the hole suddenly exists around me, and everyone else is in it with me; in reality, it is a hole without an edge, an openness. Can I write in such a way as to speak? I hope so—I am trying to do it. The poets do it, as we'll see. Barthes calls this kind of writing *writing aloud,* and distinguishes it from speech, although his description of it makes it obvious that it is energized by speech: it captures speech *close up,* he says, and makes us hear "in their materiality, their sensuality, the breath, the gutterals, the fleshiness of the lips, a whole presence of the human muzzle" (*The Pleasure of the Text,* translated by Richard Miller). Poetry returns writing to the muzzle, to the body's mouth; but of course, this is where it came from in the first place. As Heidegger puts it, language is the flower of the mouth.

Many writers go out toward the world, but find in their way an invisible film, a stickiness that they get caught in and can't break through: language. But some writers, as the best writers always have, quietly speak from their bodies, and speak the world. The best writing is energized by speech, and the best speech surges forward like a wave. Poetry is in fact such a wave. It gathers across the earth, rises up through the body of the poet, and crests in the poem. For a poem to move us, that whole wave must be implied and contained by the crest. In poetry, writing is not the same as speech, but is transformed by speech, so that language is voluptuous and contains a body, and the words literally *move,* as the first cutting edge of the wave welling up inside them.

PART II Poetry and the Body

ONE Poetry and Speech

LANGUAGE surrounds poetry with its silence and judges poetry with its attention, but language is not the essence of poetry. Poetry is a form of writing in which language has been transformed by speech. It possesses elements of language as a structure—particularly the power of words to refer to and contain other words—but these elements are transformed by the activity of speech. The misconception that language alone is the raw material of poetry has resulted in those textbook approaches to poetry that slice it up into diction, tropes, rhythm, meter, symbol, myth, etc. Because language is a static, ideal system, poetry is thought of as static as well, and is defined according to certain static ornaments of language. Poetry becomes a kind of idealized jewelry of an ideal system. But the poet is not a disembodied consciousness selecting words as if they were pearls to string on his poem. Rather, he is a real person in a concrete situation, and his words are always a product of his incarnateness, of the performance, the gesture, the act, the carving out he draws up from his environment through his body. When the poet deals with words, he is not dealing with the preexisting independent pieces of a puzzle. The actual case is completely different. Poetry, rather than being like typesetting, is a kind of reverse carving out, or a carving outward, in which the substance from which the poet carves is constantly being produced by the very gesture of carving. In this sense, poetry resembles dance more than any other art form. Just as the body in dance modulates space by carving itself outward, and thus gives space a center or focus, so speech in poetry sweeps from side to side in self-proliferating slices or layers which modulate silence, that particular silence called listening.

Language makes demands upon poetry, but these demands help us to understand language more than poetry. If we want to understand poetry, we have to recognize that speech both carries language into the ear, so that we hear it *close up* (as Barthes says in *The Pleasure of the Text*) and at the same time widens beyond language, contains language within its complex, incessant movement.

With this in mind—the primacy of speech—most of the commonplaces about poetry take on an entirely new meaning. For example, the commonplace that poetry is a "concentrated" form of expression. What does "concentrated" mean? It means that words and grammatical units are injected with a much greater potential weight and power of reference than in normal speech. But in order for this to happen, poetry must exist in a state at once both open and closed to speech. *Open to speech* means that the words and grammatical units are loosely and freely related to each other, as they are in speech. That is, in order to increase the potential of multiple reference, they must be like water molecules, capable of sliding over, beyond, or into and out of each other. Poetry, like speech, is in this sense a "mobile series of approximations," to use Barthes's phrase.

Closed to speech means that the elements of poetry repose more solidly in themselves, in that a word or phrase can carry a greater load of meanings than in speech. When speech enters poetry, it always carries with it, like a bud or seed, this power of language by which words both contain their own histories and attract other words. In this sense, poetry values the individual word more than ordinary speech. Speech displays a hasty indifference, since it is always directed at what hasn't been spoken. What has been spoken is discarded as soon as it is pounced upon. Actually, poetry does incorporate this tendency of speech too: words are always ahead of themselves, always in front of themselves, open, searching, in the mode of discovery. But in poetry, words simultaneously catch up with themselves to fill the gap they have made, so that they clog up as well as rush through the poem, and fold in on themselves, repose in themselves, at the same time that they devour themselves in sheer momentum and mobility. Poetry is not simply a "concentrated" form of speech. It is both concentrated and diluted speech, opaque and transparent speech. It is more than simply open and closed speech: it is speech that is in a permanent open-closed state, because it combines the weightlessness of seeking with the weight of what it discovers.

This open-closed state needs to be examined more closely. The attitude of discovery sharpens speech, so that it can probe, search, and pursue, but at the same time widens, dilates and softens speech, to make it receptive. Speech in poetry searches and probes, but also waits and listens. This is not the discovery of the aggressive explorer, not deliberate "clear-sighted" scientific inquiry, but the haphazard discovery of dream and reverie that drifts toward its goal, that lets itself become. There is no step-by-step process. There may be a circling around, a playing off of, even a shying away from what is to be discovered, followed by a sudden and miraculous dwelling within it:

Love bade me welcome: yet my soul drew back,
　　Guiltie of dust and sinne.
But quick-ey'd Love, observing me grow slack
　　From my first entrance in,
Drew nearer to me, sweetly questioning,
　　If I lack'd any thing.

A guest, I answer'd, worthy to be here:
　　Love said, You shall be he.
I the unkinde, ungratefull? Ah my deare,
　　I cannot look on thee.
Love took my hand, and smiling did reply,
　　Who made the eyes but I?

Truth, Lord; but I have marr'd them; let my shame
　　Go where it doth deserve.
And know you not, sayes Love, who bore the blame?
　　My deare, then I will serve.
You must sit down, sayes Love, and taste my meat.
　　So I did sit and eat.

In this poem by George Herbert, speech is mobilized in the form of discovery, with its edges spread out and its center widened, in order to listen, search, and find. When it finds, then it closes, like certain flowers: "So I did sit and eat." It's not only the preponderance of open vowels in the poem that gives it this quality of discovery, but even more the mode of existence of the speech itself. Speech in this poem moves forward with a momentum which overshoots and undershoots its mark, but which is also inevitable, that is, which is sure to be rewarded with the peace of its discovery, like a pendulum coming to a halt. This speech is more plastic than ordinary speech; it is like a mouth. There's no question of the poet's approaching speech, but rather of speech being at the service of the poet, on *his* side of the threshold of communication, like his mouth. Speech in the poem is not an intermediary, but rather a direct and immediate expression of the poet's wishes, doubts, and hesitations. This is why speech is not only the poem's medium, but its very being, and why the discovery of a truth in the poem becomes also the discovery of the poem itself.

Often in poetry this openness of speech in the mode of discovery results in an evaporation of the normal syntactical rules of speech. Speech in this condition reverts to a primitive sort of parataxis, that is, a clustering of words bridged only by contiguity, not by grammatical subordination of any kind. The line structure of poetry, by which poems are composed of repeated quanta of language laid on top of each other, lends itself particularly well to parataxis:

> Because I do not hope to turn again
> Because I do not hope
> Because I do not hope to turn
> Desiring this man's gift and that man's scope
> I no longer strive to strive toward such things
> (Why should the aged eagle stretch its wings?)
> Why should I mourn
> The vanished power of the usual reign?
>
> [T. S. Eliot, "Ash Wednesday"]

At times, grammatical subordination itself is subordinated to this speech clustering; this is what Shakespeare does with the ambiguous syntax in his sonnets, in which a line may exist in a floating relationship of subordination to either the line above or the line below it. William Empson was the first to point this out; the following is his example, taken from Sonnet 93. The third line is the ambiguous one, and can be read as subordinate to either lines two or four:

> But heaven in thy creation did decree
> That in thy face sweet love should ever dwell,
> Whate'er thy thoughts or thy heart's workings be,
> Thy looks should nothing thence, but sweetness tell.

This ability of clusters of words in poetry to detach from and attach themselves to other clusters testifies to the open, dilated state of speech in poetry, a state in which speech is at the same time more primitive and more sophisticated than in ordinary usage. More primitive in that it is less regimented, more liquid; it resides in its mobile potentialities, and holds back from the static forms that would lop off its freedom. But more sophisticated in that all of the history, all of the grammatical and syntactical possibilities of speech are gathered into this freedom.

At the same time that poetry is open in the mode of discovery, it is closed in the mode of what it discovers. The weightlessness of searching, probing, and listening, of looking into the future, exists simultaneously with the weight of speech thickening and congealing as what is discovered takes shape. This means that the word in poetry, as well as being a link between other words (as it is in speech) is also a repository (as it is in language). Speech backs up in the word as well as proceeds through it. I am thinking of words used as puns, words rooted in the structure of the language, words like jellyfish with their evolution showing. In poetry, speech transforms language, but language also thickens speech. This thickening of speech is increased as well by the effect of the proximity of words upon each other. The carving outward of poetry causes speech to appear in swaths or chunks, and a word may have its content inflated by its neighbors, as well as by the tone or voice of the poem as a whole. This inflation may open one or two words to each other, but its effect in terms of the poem as a whole is to close those words and seal them, making them opaque and heavy. Consider Shakespeare's Sonnet 129:

> Th' expense of spirit in a waste of shame
> Is lust in action; and till action, lust
> Is perjured, murderous, bloody, full of blame,
> Savage, extreme, rude, cruel, not to trust.

The words "spirit" and "expense" take on an added weight and a kind of closure in the phrase "expense of spirit," as do the words "waste" and "shame" in the phrase "waste of shame." The word "lust" is filled and sealed off by a whole string of words, "savage, extreme, rude, cruel," and so forth, which in turn are inflated by the word "lust." As a result, the lines are almost dragged down by their words, as if the words were balls attached to the chain of speech.

Still, this closed state of speech in poetry exists always within the context of the open state already described. In Shakespeare's Sonnet 129, the words may be weighted balls, but the line is still a chain, that is, a horizontal momentum. In ordinary speech, the horizontal dimension is dominant: words fly out one after the other, and meaning and intention extend over the surface of words, or rather, are pursued by that surface as it sweeps and stretches out. In poetry, this pursuit is united with the greater weight and gravity of the words. The poem falls vertically through the words at the same time that it falls in regulated tiers, in plateaus, which give the poem that same sense of pursuit, of the horizontal, that normal speech has.

This transformation of the vertical by the horizontal, the closed by the open, has a strange and beautiful effect in poetry: the vertical draws the horizontal in, but the horizontal opens the vertical, that is, pulls it upward and outward. Each dimension in poetry thus has a kind of double stress to it: a rising motion as well as a falling motion, and a tightening and gathering in as well as a thrust outward. To return to the metaphor of the dance, poetry is a kind of gesture in which weight is both carried upward and released downward, and which has no horizontal teleology to it, that is, which does not chain the horizontal to a goal on one side only, as walking does. To slightly modify Valéry's analogy, speech is like walking, but poetry, in its absence of a horizontal goal, is like dancing. Like a dance, poetry gathers in the horizontal and verticalizes it, while at the same time it spreads the vertical outward in the open form of pursuit.

Actually, this pursuit often does have a goal. Some of the best poetry takes on the reciprocal sense of speech; it listens as well as talks, it becomes energized by the presence of another. This other may be a person, a creature, a thing, a sense of place. In its absence, a poem often simply pursues itself, becomes a kind of pure act of pursuit. When we think of the experience of reading a poem, this sense of pursuit—of movement impelled by desire—becomes dominant. Our sense of time is magnified, as in a movie. In a poem, there is always a kind of continual present, a crest, with a past rapidly trailing off and disappearing behind it, and a future appearing and suddenly rising toward it. This is a kind of reverse sagging, by which the line contracts toward the word, which itself exists at the peak of the crest. This falling and rising motion is similar to the rising up before us and the falling behind us of a landscape as we walk through it. The line structure of poetry lends itself especially well to this effect. Poetry is a discontinuous continuity, a kind of pulsing, in which successive quanta of speech are laid on top of each other in such a way that the vertical column of lines is opened up by the horizontal series of words. Formal poetry regularizes the discontinuity by layering equal quantities of speech; but all poetry, if it is poetry, achieves this transformation of the vertical by the horizontal.

Yeats, for example: in "Leda and the Swan," the line is exploding outward while the words are driving themselves inward and downward. There is a simultaneous implosion and explosion, a violent insertion of the poem into itself, and a struggle of the poem to be free of itself (and free of the sonnet form). Of course, this activity is reflected thematically as well.

A sudden blow: the great wings beating still
Above the staggering girl, her thighs caressed
By the dark webs, her nape caught in his bill,
He holds her helpless breast upon his breast.

How can those terrified vague fingers push
The feathered glory from her loosening thighs?
And how can body, laid in that white rush,
But feel the strange heart beating where it lies?

A shudder in the loins engenders there
The broken wall, the burning roof and tower
and Agamemnon dead.

            Being so caught up,
So mastered by the brute blood of the air,
Did she put on his knowledge with his power
Before the indifferent beak could let her drop?

The multiple meanings of such words as "shudder," "knowledge," and "power," the vertical correspondence between
words like "blow," "holds," "push," "beating," and "put" on
the one hand, and "staggering," "helpless," "terrified," "mastered," and "indifferent" on the other, and the references to a
personal myth system, all serve to give the words a vertical
thickness or weight. At the same time, the enjambment that
lends a breathless momentum to the line, the occasional
"springing" of the rhythm that widens the line and reinforces
its conversational quality, and the half-rhymes that struggle
outward against the form, all serve to explode the poem hori-
zontally, as if it were trying to fling its arms apart. The result is
that, even while they are drawn in by the words, the lines fly
apart, and even while they plunge downward, the words are
pulled up and out by the lines. This poem by Yeats, whose form
is both a straitjacket and a springboard, whose speech is vio-
lently contending against itself, but whose violence always
moves outward, on the outer edge of control, is a radical exam-

ple of what happens in all poetry. Before we even begin to understand the poem rationally, we become aware of it as pursuit and desire, unmediated, as in a dance. The dance, of course, is an analogy that Yeats himself used in other poems, and that is implicit in the strange pas de deux of "Leda and the Swan." In dance, we are aware of the body as a body, while we simultaneously witness its drawing up out of itself, its self-transcendence that causes gravity to be subject to the body instead of vice versa. Similarly, in poetry, speech has the closedness and opacity, even the fleshiness of the body, while it transcends itself in the mode of pursuit.

When speech enters poetry it brings with it a desire to find, to seek. Then poetry closes around speech and thickens it, turns it back upon itself and gives it a weight and opacity it normally lacks. Speech is an act of the body, but it normally escapes the body into the air and disappears, leaving no residue, not even a track. Poetry inserts the extension and gravity of the body back into speech. At the same time, the body brings into poetry its tendency to describe weightless gestures, to dance. Speech in poetry is open and closed in the same way the body is open and closed, as a column of flesh that is also a well or cave, an opening out of the world as well as a projection onto it.

TWO Poetry and the Body

NOT ONLY IS my body the means by which I exist in the world, and not only does the thickness of my body enable me to apprehend the thickness of the world, but also my very experience of synthesis, of an arrangement of parts and whole in the things around me, is grounded in my body. Since I possess a "body image" by means of which my whole body is present in each of my gestures, it is only natural that I should see integrated wholes in the world in terms of my body. We say the legs of the chair, the arms of the clock, and so on. But a bookcase also presents a distant but readable bodily appearance, as does an ashtray, a refrigerator, a jug, a tree, a river, and so on; these things are read as having torsos or trunks, limbs or organs, and often heads or hearts, that is, centers.

Furthermore, this duplication of the body occurs upon the body itself. The hand, the foot, the penis are all miniature bodies; Rodin's hand sculptures, as Rilke pointed out, express entire bodily gestures, such as sleeping, waking, fatigue, the loss of desire. Even the mouth is a kind of body; the teeth are its skeleton, the lips its skin, and the tongue is the expressive power of its limbs, distilled into a drop that exists below the threshold of any particular limb. It's appropriate, then, to regard poems, which are born in the mouth, which are gestures of the body, themselves as bodies. As with Rodin's hand sculptures, there are poems that describe entire bodily gestures; some are awkward and adolescent, but with a brash expansiveness (Rimbaud), some are graceful, thin, and lithe (William Carlos Williams) or sensual and trumped up (Dylan Thomas), and some are spare, lean, and tight, as well as too elusive and solitary ever to completely disclose themselves (W. S. Merwin). The style of a poet is nothing more than the personality expressed in his bodily gestures; since poems themselves are bodily gestures, they will naturally express this personality as well as the way the poet dresses or lights his cigarette. But since poems are bodies themselves, they will also express their own unique personalities, related to but distinct from the poet's. It is true that the poet speaks the poem, but the poem also speaks itself, and this is because it is a body.

When the poem speaks itself, sound is its mouth, the opening out of which it sings and bodies forth. And sound is the language with which poems dress themselves, the language of gestures that enables them to construct their own separate personalities. This is because sounds themselves are bodies; syllables can be sleepy, vulgar, prudish, withered, lazy, moist, heavy. Phonemes themselves have bodily characteristics; as Rousseau pointed out, the vowels express passions and the consonants needs. According to Wellek and Warren, the front vowels (*e* and *i*) express thin, clear, bright things, and the back vowels (*o* and *u*) dark, clumsy, slow, dull things; the dentals (*d* and *t*) express firmness, and the labials (*b*, *p*, *m*) suppleness, flexibility. Edmond Jabès says that words themselves "are bodies whose members are letters. Their sex is always a vowel" (cited in Bachelard, *The Poetics of Reverie*). Through this lan-

guage of bodies, the poem describes its own bodily gesture, its
own dance and dumb show of speech and song. When we read
a poem we activate this inner drama of shapes and syllables.
Consider the following passage by Theodore Roethke:

> On things asleep, no balm!
> A kingdom of stinks and sighs,
> Fetor of cockroaches, dead fish, petroleum,
> Worse than castoreum of mink or weasels,
> Saliva dripping from warm microphones,
> agony of crucifixion on barstools.

At first the sounds are heavy and dormant; they have to wake
up in our mouth, or rather, wake our mouth up, and gradually
they do. The languor of the broad *o* in the first and third lines
becomes invaded by the strident, nervous short *i*'s of line two,
and the seductive liquid and labial *l*'s, *r*'s, *p*'s, and *m*'s of line
three. The dominant gesture is one of thickness and weight; if
the poem speaks, it speaks like a recording played at slow
speed; if it dances, it dances with heavy, sleepy legs. But this
thickness and weight metamorphoses into other shapes and
gestures, and the closer we look at the poem the more quickly
and almost randomly it changes. Consider line four, "Worse
than castoreum of mink or weasels." Read it not as a collection
of words, but as a collection of sounds. The elephantine
pirouette of *wor* ends in the hiss of a serpent, *se*, which gradually glides, as the tongue inches forwards, into the lisp of *th*.
These sounds are posing for us; they are mocking us and trying
to seduce us at the same time. But the lisp evaporates into the
broad *an* of "than," and the line opens up as if its exaggerated
dance were a joke. The *c* kicks its foot lightheartedly. But *as*,
although open and exposed, echoes the hiss of the serpent, and
tor once again melts into the full and blowsy pose of a seducer,
only this time with more of a Prussian authority and weight to
it. *Eum* is its song, the formula tune with which it calls up and

exposes its appetite (as in "fe fi fo fum"). But *of* is the inadequacy of that appetite, *m* is its closing off, and *ink* is the shrinkage of the line back into the leering pose of a serpent. *Or*, sandwiched between *ink* and *wea*, is a hint of former fullness, a last attempt to regain the stature of *tor*, but *wea* is that stature reduced to childishness, and *sels* is its final pinched laugh, a bow and a scrape, an embarrassed attempt to mollify the reader before the next attack in the next line. These syllables that glide into and out of each other, as a dancer glides into and out of her various limbs, are the body of the poem as it performs its dance, an eclectic, protean dance that eventually incorporates every conceivable human gesture, including the most noble and the most shameful ones. The poem is drunk with the possibilities of its bodily language and trying as rapidly as it can to exhaust them all; it is possessed by these possibilities, as if they were rushing through its body, seizing it with their personalities, and releasing it like a puppet, only to seize it again. This dance is one in which expression makes use of the dancer, rather than vice versa, and in which the body has become the face of expression, the immediate and naked surging up of expression into the world.

Poems are bodies. They are drops that break off from the mass of a poet's body, congeal, take shape, and become bodies themselves. When a poem speaks, it speaks with its entire body, not only with its voice, but with its rhythm, pace, shape, and tone, as well as its denotative content. What I have described with regard to sound, that is, with regard to the poem's mouth, takes place across the whole body of the poem as well; the form of the poem is the form of an elaborate, completed bodily gesture, a complex bodily ritual, which ideally encompasses a great deal of variety, as in the Roethke line, but which also will return to certain gestures and evolve a more general pattern out of their repetition. Lorca's poem "Your Childhood in Menton" is a perfect example of this. The following is a translation (by Edwin Honig), and so leaves behind, of course, the original voice of the poem, the gesture of its sounds. But the gesture of its repetitions is fully preserved, as well as the dance of its pace and tone; these constitute, in fact, a large part of the content of the poem, since the words have been stripped as much as possible of their denotative power in order to liberate their expressiveness:

> Yes, your childhood now a legend of fountains.
> The train, and the woman who fills the sky.
> Your evasive solitude in hotels
> and your pure mask of another sign.
> It is the sea's childhood and the silence
> where wisdom's glasses all are shattered.
> It is your inert ignorance of where
> my torso lay, bound by fire.
> Man of Apollo, I gave you love's pattern,
> the frenzied nightingale's lament.
> But, pasture of ruins, you kept lean
> for brief and indecisive dreams.
> Thought of what was confronted, yesterday's light,
> tokens and traces of chance.
> Your restless waist of sand
> favors only tracks that don't ascend.
> But I must search all corners
> for your tepid soul without you which doesn't understand you
> with my thwarted Apollonian sorrow
> that broke through the mask you wear.
> There, lion, there, heavenly fury,
> I'll let you graze on my cheeks;
> there, blue horse of my madness,
> pulse of nebula and minute hand,
> I'll search the stones for scorpions
> and your childlike mother's clothes,
> midnight lament and ragged cloth
> that tore the moon out of the dead man's brow.
> Yes, your childhood now a legend of fountains.

Soul a stranger to my veins' emptiness,
I'll search for you rootless and small.
Eternal love, love, love that never was!
Oh, yes! I love. Love, love! Leave me.
Don't let them gag me, they who seek
the wheat of Saturn through the snow,
who castrate creatures in the sky,
clinic and wilderness of anatomy.
Love, love, love. Childhood of the sea.
Your tepid soul without you which doesn't understand you.
Love, love, a flight of deer
through the endless heart of whiteness.
And your childhood, love, your childhood.
The train, and the woman who fills the sky.
Not you or I, not the wind or the leaves.
Yes, your childhood now a legend of fountains.

This is poetry as pure expression, as a bodily dance that leaps forward and back, stops, slows down, frantically lashes out, becomes weary or ironic, soothes and placates, and finally winds up where it began, after sculpting an entire world of human gestures, a perfectly trim and supple world with no excess and no lack. Lorca's poem is an extreme and beautiful example of the body entering speech, as it does in all poetry, and filling it with its expressiveness, its disclosures, its tone, grace, tempo, modulation, and so forth. Poetry is speech metamorphosed by the body, a dance of sound in which the words are so expressive and charged with tone that they wake up to each other and their mutual possibilities, and like arms and legs, describe a little ballet of opposition and reconciliation, of independence and community. Speech in this state becomes completely and immediately expressive, without any intermediary explanations or systems of signs; it becomes like a face, a natural language, with no gap between sign and signified. This is why beginners are reluctant to show their poems to others, because they are so embarrassingly naked, like faces. Like a face, a poem

gathers itself up and becomes weightless, that is, wholly present not in its substance but in what that substance expresses.
Or rather, this substance becomes modulated and distributed
according to the attitudes, poses, gestures of that face; it becomes a kind of variable content that will be sculpted by the
dance of the face, its expression.

The notion of a poem being a face should dispel the problem
of form and content. The form of a face is inseparable from its
content, just as its expression is inseparable from what it expresses; this is true of a poem as well. One of the rituals of
contemporary criticism is to talk about the inseparability of
form and content in literature. This is a sort of rite of passage
that, once performed, allows the critic then to go ahead and talk
about form and content in the way he wanted in the first place:
as if they were separable. In fact, if form is conceived as an
external shape or outline on the one hand, or an internal idea or
purpose on the other, then it already is separated from content.
But form is none of these. Form is rather a certain condition or
state of being; in the case of the body, a condition of liberation
from its utilitarian activities and in general from its dead
weight. But it is not the form which is liberated; it is the entire
body. If the aim of dance is to release the form trapped in the
body, this is the same as releasing the body itself. Releasing it
from what? From the grip things have on it, the grip of clothing,
furniture, taxes, work, and the earth itself. When the body takes
on form it takes on a kind of self-realized freedom.

This is true of poetry as well. When the poem takes on form it
takes on independence; one's feelings are set free, words are set
free, the world is set free, and the poem is set free. From now on
they're on their own. The form of a poem evaporates as soon as
the poem is born, as soon as the poem takes on its own autonomous freedom, its own body. If any residue of form is left,
then the poem has two bodies, neither of which quite fits into

the other. It becomes like a face with two skins, or a dancer with a heavy suit of clothes, which, instead of being absorbed into her gestures, weighs upon them, and even dislodges them from their intended arc. Form is a condition of self-reference of content, or rather, is a kind of self-reference that is also completely open, like a face. When speech enters poetry, what we call form is really a body, but a self-sustaining and self-delighting body, like a face:

> Whenas in silks my Julia goes,
> Then, then, methinks, how sweetly flows
> That liquefaction of her clothes.
>
> Next, when I cast mine eyes, and see
> That brave vibration each way free;
> O, how that glittering taketh me!

The body of this poem by Herrick is severed from the grip of burdensome things and drawn up into itself. At the same time, it is completely exposed to the reader, like a face whose expression has stolen up on it and taken it by surprise. There is no question here of a form into which a content is poured, but rather of a form whose content or substance is born with it, and gathered up into its act of being born. This doesn't mean, however, that things—even burdensome ones—aren't present in the poem. Rather, it means that they've been transformed: "clothes" in the poem are at the same time both more and less real than clothes in the world. They are clothes ritualized by language and the body, clothes named for the first time ("That liquefaction of her clothes") and therefore clothes whose existence has been renewed.

In other words, speech in poetry, in addition to being expressive, also points out things and names them. This is the difference between poetry and music or dance, despite all their similarities. In music and dance, expression is an open form that disappears as soon as it is propelled forward, whereas in poetry, expression, as soon as it opens up from the body, closes upon the thing it names. In music and dance, expression never leaves itself, but in poetry, expression carries a sediment that rides on the crest of the act of expression and is left in the world when that crest disappears. This sediment is the name of something. Those who assert that speech can be only denotative on the one hand (as in science) or expressive on the other (as in poetry) are selling poetry short. Speech may fragment itself when it is used technologically, but when it is used poetically it heals itself, so that denotation and expression, which are normally treated as separate in our culture, come together and regain their original unity, and denotation becomes a form of expression, while expression itself names.

This is simply another way of saying that just as speech bridges the spectrum that has gestures, faces, etc., on one end, and language, numbers, etc., on the other, so poetry bridges the same spectrum. But poetry also tries to bring the two ends of the spectrum together: to drive gesture into meaning and meaning into gesture in such a way that they are indistinguishable, and become Novalis's "natural" language, or what Norman O. Brown calls the language of Adam. I think poetry does this by recovering with the gestures of speech one of the primary functions of language, one of the first things language must do in organizing the world: naming.

THREE Poetry and World: Naming

SO FAR, we've followed poetry like a spiral from its disappearing point which is also its root in the mouth, through its being in speech, into its form as a body. Now we come to its outermost curve, the gesture that lodges in the world by taking up and naming things. In front of us are these creatures called names: desk, pencil, window, sky. But what are they? They are not descriptions of something. A description translates the visual appearance of a thing into the conventions of language; there is a distance inserted into all descriptions, a distance that results from the act of translating something from one language (its visual appearance) into another (language itself). In naming, this distance disappears; there is no translation, because language itself is not presupposed. Rather, language comes into existence. The tension that exists between language and the world exists for the purpose of naming things. When we name, language lodges in the world like a hook, and brings things forward; yet, it releases them at the same time. Language organizes the world—the world resists language. When it names things, language impregnates and clarifies the world at the same time that the world, clarified, sheds language.

First of all, a name penetrates a thing and brings it forth so that it can be handled by language, so that language will have a world to avail itself of. A name is not identical with the essence of something, but it does extract that essence so that we can deal with it. Essence means not only substance or identity, but the source of power of something. Names tap this source of power, as in the Rumplestiltskin story. We name things in order to gain access over them, so that we can invoke them, call them up in our presence when we want to. Like children who have learned their mother's name, and must call her in order to test our power, we want things to be our servants, to be under our power, and naming gives us this privilege.

But in addition to enslaving things, names also set things free, release them. When I name something I give it a form, the form of the name, a certain shape in my mouth. I give it a part of me; I fragment myself and attach some of my power to that thing. Once named, it has a new autonomy, a new freedom. It has achieved a kind of closure outside of me and has become itself. Naming confirms things in their essences, actualizes them; if you take away my name, I can be anyone. If by naming something we gain a power over it, the power that we gain is the power of that thing's autonomy and freedom, its actualization. Naming clarifies the world, so that it has variety and distinctness, and we can walk around in it on equal terms, with beings that exist to the left and right, instead of wading through a swamp that resists us with its homogeneous thickness. This is why Adam named the animals. We are creatures who designate, who denote, who separate things and give them names, and then give names to the relationships between those things, and between them and us. We have to do this; it's the destiny of our language and bodies, both so perfectly suited to encompassing things, passing among them, picking them up, turning them over, holding them to the light. Naming grants things the power of our bodies, the power of being open and closed to each other; once named, things are able to resemble or contrast, to be in relations of sympathy and antipathy, cause and effect, and so on. If things didn't have names, we would be absorbed in them. In the act of naming, there is such a transfer of power that objects are given the value of subjects. Naming is our discourse with objects, and names are their mode of speech. When I say "tree," I am giving the tree access to me. I have gained a certain power over the tree, but it has gained a power over me as well, since now I need it to complete my existence. If the tree refuses my name, if it holds back, if it doesn't respond to my summons, then a vacuum exists, the tree has become conspicuous, obstinate, and opaque, and I've become subject to its mute dominance. Its false name sits inertly in my mouth and can't be spit out, like so much debris. Just as at one time the tree needed me in order for its existence to be confirmed, so now I need the tree in order for my body to be confirmed, in order for the shape in my mouth to have an issue, to bear fruit, rather than to pass coldly by the tree and remain barren.

Naming calls things forth. But how often do they come? That depends upon whether language is naming or poetry is naming. We need poetry because names die, because objects resist their names, because the world overflows and escapes its names. Names die because they are tamed by habit; they become mere sounds, and call up habitual responses rather than the essence of the things they name. The name "tree" calls up a hackneyed picture, or more, an attitude toward a hackneyed picture, and this enables us to dispose of the actual tree and forget about it. Does the name "tree" evoke the reality of a tree for you? Does the tree rise up in front of you as if for the first time? Can you see and feel the corrugated texture of the bark, the depth of green and yellow in the leaves, the scar just below the first limb? In fact, the name "tree," although it may be sufficient for everyday practical discourse, as in "cut down

three hundred trees today," doesn't do the job of truly extract-
ing and calling forth the essence of a tree for the person who
says it.

Part of the problem is that the name is too wide or general. By
saying "tree," I haven't really named this being in front of me,
but a certain category, part of a larger taxonomic system that
exists as a kind of mental architecture inside me; I have referred
as much if not more to a system of human meanings and its
possibilities than to this being before me. "Sycamore" would
reduce the breadth of this system somewhat, but not to the skin
of this object, *this* sycamore. To name a thing with language is
to allow that thing to shed language and to allow the world to
collect beyond language. No language has a name for everything; otherwise it would truly be a language of Babel. Only
poetry attempts to name things completely in their individuality, to give them their individuality. If I want to know what this
tree in front of me is, this sycamore, this "Young Sycamore,"
then I turn to poetry:

> I must tell you
> this young tree
> whose round and firm trunk
> between the wet
>
> pavement and the gutter
> (where water
> is trickling) rises
> bodily
>
> into the air with
> one undulant
> thrust half its height—
> and then
>
> dividing and waning
> sending out
> young branches on
> all sides—

hung with cocoons
it thins
till nothing is left of it
but two

eccentric knotted
twigs
bending forward
hornlike at the top

(William Carlos Williams, "Young Sycamore")

When poetry names, it is not the same as language naming. Poetry is not a taxonomy; it is at once narrower and wider than language; narrower in that it names this particular sycamore tree, to the exclusion of all others, and wider in that anything in the world, previous to classifications, is potential subject matter for poetry. Language extends over a certain area and plunges only to a certain depth. What is below this depth? Everything. Language ranges over things, infuses the world, but at the same time shuns the particular.

This particular that language shuns does not include only trees, pineapples, doors, and panthers; it does not include only physical beings. It includes relationships between beings, and it includes our feelings about them. The weakest area of language, the area in which it helplessly has at its disposal only one or two blankets to cover thousands of sleeping beings, is the area of feelings. Our names for feelings are far too crude; there are few if any feelings that we can call "love," "hate," "sadness," "joy." Just as Mallarmé asserted that a line of poetry is in a sense a new word, so an entire poem, when it concerns a feeling—which would include all poetry—comprises a new name, the name of that feeling that has never before been named, perhaps because it has never before existed. What are piety and exhilaration doing together in a poem? They are together because the feeling the poem names exists previous to

the clumsy, unmodulated, slablike words "piety" and "exhilaration." These names are like a piece of marble before it has
been sculpted; the poem is the sculpture itself, the finished
name in its complete individuality, incapable of being translated into any other words:

> My heart leaps up when I behold
>   A rainbow in the sky:
> So was it when my life began;
> So is it now I am a man;
> So be it when I shall grow old,
>   Or let me die!
> The Child is father of the Man;
> And I could wish my days to be
> Bound each to each by natural piety.
>
> (Wordsworth, "My Heart Leaps Up When I Behold")

The feelings we describe with the names "piety" and "exhilaration" exist in exactly the same relation to this poem as the name
"tree" exists to the poem by William Carlos Williams. They are
like loose mental tents erected around the thing; but the poem
itself is lodged in the very center of the thing, so that the proper
order of being is restored, and the thing is previous to its
categories rather than vice versa.

Names in language are too wide or crude. The irony of this is
that they are not wide enough to really contain the essences of
things. The world always resists and overflows its names, and
language is powerless to block its escape. Indeed, in everyday
speech, names are usually tools, and speech passes through
them to something on the other side, some end or function for
which the named thing is intended. "Cut down three hundred
trees today" means cut them down so I can sell them for fifty
dollars a cord. Meanwhile, the essence of the tree has hardly
been touched. Poetry attempts to catch up with this essence that
is trying to escape, to capture it for a moment before it over-

flows for good. The best poems capture the thing on the verge
of spilling out of its name. Here is "Archaic Torso of Apollo" by
Rilke:

> We never saw his fantastic head
> where the eye-apples ripened. But
> his torso shines like a candlelabrum
> and his gaze like an ember survives
>
> and glows. Otherwise the curve
> of the chest wouldn't twist in a smile
> and dip to the burning center of love.
>
> Otherwise, the transparent plunge of the
> shoulders would suddenly end deformed
> and the stone wouldn't gleam like animal skin
>
> and break out from its sharp edges
> like a star: here there is no place
> that doesn't see you. You must change your life.

This archaic torso is overflowing its name, which is the poem
itself, into something it once was, into general animate nature,
and finally, into a moral imperative. There is no question here
of speech passing through the name into an end or function on
the other side; rather, speech jams up in the name, and the
name itself is lodged in the thing, in its undeniable presence,
around or through which there is no path. If there is an end or
function, the thing seizes it and tosses it back to the one doing
the naming: "You must change your life." This archaic torso
tells us what all properly named things tell us: that the name
focuses the thing, but the thing will eventually escape its name,
since its power, a power that it seizes at least in part from the
namer, is greater than the mere word that awakens it.

Yet, that mere word, or series of words, does awaken it. It
awakens and opens it up, and the sheer majesty that pours out
is more than it bargained for. The word went in search of a
name; this happens in all poetry. This is what it means for

speech in poetry to be in the mode of discovery. Why did the word search for a name? Because the name already in use was weak or impotent; the thing had shed it because it was inadequate. But unfortunately, the thing was unable to stand forth without it. Since it had no name, although it tried to appear, it could produce no inner light and was in danger of escaping into nothingness. Are we talking about a "real" torso here? It doesn't matter. We are talking about a reality. We could say it is a linguistic torso, the body of a poem, and that the poem, like so many other modern poems, is about itself. Certainly, it is about something that we were unable to see, that existed in a kind of cloudiness or murkiness on the verge of annihilation. We were unable to see it because we had no name for it. Our speech had only a certain limited number of names at its disposal, and these were too wide or crude to rescue it. It had already half disappeared when the poet finally approached it: "We never saw his fantastic head." The poet took up our inadequate speech and set it struggling against itself, to transform it into something more delicately modulated; he carved away, carved outward, in order to arrive at a name that would reawaken the thing by permeating it and filling it out. But this process was fruitless; the name couldn't fill the thing, because the thing expanded as it was named. Finally, it exploded, "broke out from its sharp edges," and overflowed its name, overflowed the realm of speech, and overflowed the niche of contemplative space in which speech had tried to place it. This overflowing is still going on. It is a powerful wave that carries the namer with it, until both he and the thing find themselves in the strange and new realm of action and moral responsibility, the realm that draws poetry toward it at the same time that it leaves it behind: "You must change your life."

Three Poems in Their Bodies

ONE Donne's Holy Sonnet XIV

I'D LIKE TO BEGIN talking about Donne's "Batter my heart" sonnet by making some general remarks about language in the Elizabethan age. My description at the end of Part I of language as an object in our culture may become more clear if we look at a culture for which language was not an object, because there was no contradiction between language and speech. Northrup Frye calls the fascination of the Elizabethans with words a reverse drunkenness: the more that poured out, the giddier they became. In fact, speech for the Elizabethans not only drew upon language, as speech always does, but was engaged in the act of creating it as well. Furthermore, because new words entered the language everyday, that language itself was engaged in the act of creating the world around the Elizabethans. So there was an intimacy between words and things that we lack in a culture whose language has been reified and made self-sufficient, a thing in itself.

This intimacy was involved with a much-discussed belief of the Elizabethans, their tendency to see correspondences between things. The Elizabethans created a world of correspondences with a language that manifests the same kinds of correspondences. A good way to experience that world is to read and participate in its language. Here is the opening quatrain of Donne's poem:

> Batter my heart, three person'd God; for, you
> As yet but knocke, breathe, shine, and seeke to mend;
> That I may rise, and stand, o'erthrow mee,'and bend
> Your force, to breake, blowe, burn and make me new.

The most striking thing about these words is the tremendous desire they contain. They also have a shattered, haphazard effect, as if they were wading through their own debris. This is partly because most of them are monosyllabic, contain short vowels (extremely sharp ones in the fourth line) and begin and end with consonants. So they are almost islands of words, but at the same time, islands called out of their isolation by longing and desire. One manifestation of this desire exists in the verbs. Most of the words in the passage are verbs, and most of the verbs transitive verbs; but there is only one object mentioned: "my heart." So there is an excess of actions in relation to objects, as if all these verbs were seeking an object to couple up with and transform.

The other manifestation of this desire lies in the repetitions of sound—alliteration, assonance, half rhyme, parallel syntax, and rhyme. This is where the idea of correspondences comes in. In the Elizabethan age, not only did words rhyme, but things rhymed too. A glowworm, for example, was defined not only according to his position in the order of creation, but also according to the other objects in creation he resembled; in this case, a comet. This resemblance is more than a resemblance: a glowworm in his own realm *is* a comet, but a comet appropriate to that realm. The same is true of correspondences between the eagle and the sun, a man's bones and rocks, his veins and rivers, his head and the king, his feet and peasants. A corollary of this idea is that things yearn to be united with their echoes. This is particularly true when applied to the four elements; fire tends to rise because it wants to be one with the sun. Similarly, our souls go out of us when we die because they want to be reunited with God. Many of Donne's poems, especially his early love lyrics, are about people and things who yearn for each other because one contains an image of the other. This happens, for example, when lovers see each other's faces in each other's eyes. A more elaborate example of it occurs in "A Valediction: Of My Name in the Window":

> The rafters of my body, bone
> Being still with you, the Muscle, Sinew, and Veine,
> Which tile this house, will come againe.

Here, "the rafters of my body" (the skeleton) refers to the poet's name, which he has scratched into his mistress's window. The name is so involved with his body, that the muscles, sinews, and veins yearn to be united with it, and will be.

Of course, this is an elaborate and humorous conceit. But it reveals three important aspects of the Elizabethan world: first, that everything has its echo or echoes; second, that things long to be united with their echoes; and third, that language and words are implanted in this world of echoes and correspondences. Language and things inhabit one space, not two, and this is a space bent across desire and sympathy. This is partly because the world of physical things for the Elizabethans is itself a kind of language, not only in the sense that things can rhyme, but in the sense that nature is a system of signs, overflowing with meaning and significance. The Elizabethans often referred to nature as a book or hieroglyph.

This is the context the poem establishes for us: there is no gap between words and things. Words *are* things, not transparent windows, but names etched in windows. Rhymes and other repetitions of sound are part of the system of correspondences—rhymes—of things in the world. I am talking about my experience of the poem, and how, approaching it, the first thing I see is that my experience is locked into a culture that may not be mine, but is made accessible for me by the words of the poem. That culture exists in the landscape of those words, in their visceral energy, the way they charge their own space with desire and longing. The words are like creatures seeking their own images, listening for their echoes. "Batter" searches through "knocke, breathe, shine," for its echo, but finds these too weak and distant. But it does find an echo in the fourth line, in the same words that "knocke, breathe, shine" find their echo in: "breake, blowe, burn." There is a similar correspondence between "Seeke to mend," and "make me new," between "breathe" and "seeke," between "stand," "mend," and "bend," and of course between the rhymes. These words are brought into fullness by desire, like fire that longs to be one with the sun.

In the terminology of Part Two, the poem is both open and closed, open in its yearning and desire, and closed in the way that desire is lodged in mirror images, echoes. Gradually, as we read the poem, these echoes begin to take on an added importance:

> Batter my heart, three person'd God; for, you
> As yet but knocke, breathe, shine, and seeke to mend;
> That I may rise, and stand, o'erthrow mee,'and bend
> Your force, to breake, blowe, burn and make me new.
> I, like an usurpt towne, to'another due,
> Labour to'admit you, but Oh, to no end,
> Reason your viceroy in mee, mee should defend,
> But is captiv'd, and proves weake or untrue,
> Yet dearely'I love you, and would be lov'd faine,
> But am bethroth'd unto your enemie

In these lines, we begin to realize the poem is becoming a sonnet. The correspondences, echoes, and yearning of words for each other, are in the process of being gathered into that overall pattern which we know by the name of "sonnet." In a sonnet, words struggle to unite with each other, especially rhyming words, but are prevented from doing so by interposed words and lines, themselves struggling to unite with others. So the poem becomes a series of blockages and passages, an elaborate structure with a narrow conduit inside. Its medium is desire, but it resolves that desire through its inevitability. This inevitability is a two-edged sword. On the one hand it derives from a kind of conservation of form. A poet can't "make up" a sonnet; he has to *enter* it. On the other hand, once he enters it he has to forget it, and allow the sonnet's gestures to become his own, like the courtier who follows prescribed manners spontaneously. Donne wasn't a "naked" poet; he couldn't have conceived of spontaneity taking its own shape, as it does for Whitman. In the Elizabethan age, because ceremony had to seem spontaneous and natural, the opposite was also true: spontaneity found its chief expression in ceremony. Ceremonies, rituals, and prescribed forms were more than a clothing Donne's culture wore; they were the very body of that culture. That is, the body was assimilated into them, like a body that becomes the clothing it wears. The Elizabethans loved a world of ceremony, because ceremony held desire in check, desire always on the verge of spilling, like wine from a glass, or verbs from a sonnet.

In this respect, the marvelous thing about a sonnet is that it *has* to complete its gesture; so the words don't really become themselves until they call up the ones they've been yearning for. This is another way of saying that in addition to being a thing, a sonnet is an act, an act that unfolds against its own resistance. But it can't afford to be impatient. In Donne's sonnet, the first four lines are so desperate and urgent that they almost outstrip the sonnet they speak through. Although it takes us perhaps a line or two to notice it, the next six lines by contrast are extremely calm. The poem seems to be trying to achieve a balance, to unfold through its desire, but to rest within itself at the same time:

> I, like an usurpt towne, to'another due,
> Labour to'admit you, but Oh, to no end,
> Reason your viceroy in mee, mee should defend,
> But is captiv'd, and proves weake or untrue,
> Yet dearely'I love you, and would be lov'd faine,
> But am betroth'd unto your enemie

The poem here is calm because, among other things, the verbs have lost a lot of their power, are almost deflated. There are no verbs in the fifth line, for the first time in the poem. In the sixth line, "Labour to'admit" indicates a passive bodily stance. First, the sonnet was labouring to free itself, to break out of its confined space; now, it's labouring to admit something else. And now most of the verbs are passive too: "is captiv'd," "be loved," "am bethroth'd." Also, the vowels are longer, and the words are not quite so jammed together as in the first four lines. There is desire in these words, but now the desire is more generalized, more spread out across the lines rather than exploding in each separate word. In fact, three lines in a row begin with "but" or "yet," as if each were dissatisfied with what it has found. Still, the poem is more patient now. Once it found itself becoming a sonnet, it calmed down in order to let itself fill, pool up, accumulate. This accumulation takes place across the entire body of the poem. But it is never really finished, in the sense of something filled and held in, completed and sealed. At the very moment the poem achieves itself, it also lets itself go, and the accumulation at its fullest turns out to be a pure kind of waiting, an incompletion held at its brink:

> Batter my heart, three person'd God; for, you
> As yet but knocke, breathe, shine, and seeke to mend;

That I may rise, and stand, o'erthrow mee,'and bend
Your force, to breake, blowe, burn and make me new.
I, like an usurpt towne, to'another due,
Labour to'admit you, but Oh, to no end,
Reason your viceroy in mee, mee should defend,
But is captiv'd, and proves weake or untrue,
Yet dearely'I love you, and would be lov'd faine,
But am betroth'd unto your enemie,
Divorce mee,'untie, or breake that knot againe,
Take me to you, imprison mee, for I
Except you'enthrall mee, never shall be free,
Nor ever chast, except you ravish mee.

Once again, in the last four lines, the poem expresses desire; these lines are similar to the opening lines, in that they begin in the imperative voice. But their desire is more a ground swell or wave building up within the words as a whole. This ground swell is sustained and held at the end of the poem resting within itself, yet about to break open. At the end, the poem is both filled, and still lacking; being filled for it is still a state of need, and so it is filled in the mode of waiting: filled with this need. Another way of saying this is that the poem is intensely reciprocal, but at the same time never sure if it will in fact *be* reciprocated. It is a form of writing opened up by a strong sense of the Other; but its energy derives in part at least from a simultaneous doubt that the Other exists, and a desire for it to exist. The poem is waiting for a reply. This expected reply—which becomes silence once the poem is over—is both something the poem approaches and the need and desire lodged in the words of the poem. As the desire gathers momentum at the end of the poem, the precipice it has been approaching comes closer and closer. When they finally meet, the poem achieves itself, in the sense of setting itself free, cutting itself adrift. But this is an uneasy freedom, because it exists entirely in the mode of waiting. The final couplet is a perfect image of this:

> Except you'enthrall me, never shall be free,
> Nor ever chast, except you ravish mee.

First of all, the verbs here are both active and passive—"enthrall," "ravish," and "be free," be "chast." They balance each other off by a kind of cross-reference, and the cross-reference is reinforced by parallel phrases. These parallel phrases have traditional names, which Donne, as an educated man, would have known. They are: anadiplosis, in which the last words of one sentence or phrase are repeated at the beginning of the next; epanalepsis, in which a sentence begins and ends with the same words or phrase; and epanodos, in which a sentence or phrase is repeated in reverse order.

A word about rhetorical devices: Donne used them consciously, especially in his Sermons and Devotions. In the Elizabethan age, rhetorical devices gave to formal speech, especially sermons, the same kind of tension and thickening that Donne secures in this poem by the sonnet form and by the use of delayed echoes of words. Rhetorical devices gave to writing some of the persuasive power and immediacy of speech, and at the same time rescued formal speech from its transcience and perishability, by folding it back on itself in a complex series of internal correspondences, parallels, and repetitions.

In the poem, this folding back of speech by means of cross-parallels makes the couplet almost self-sufficient and seemingly detachable from the rest of the poem. The sounds of the four key words in the couplet reinforce these cross-parallels: "enthrall" and "ravish" have a similar lush consonantal texture and muted vowel sound, while "free" and "chast" have a similar sharpness and bite:

> Except you'enthrall mee, never shall be free,
> Nor ever chast, except you ravish mee.

However, the seeming balance and self-sufficiency of the couplet is thrown off by the weight of one of those key words, "ravish." We respond of course to the shock of its meaning. But we respond to this shock only in and through the sound and texture, the *body*, of the word. After the long, languid drawl of "enthrall," the quick sting of "free," and the crisp, bright, but almost overbearingly cheerful face of "chast," "ravish" comes up from a subterranean passage, a word almost disemboweled, a rag of a word with hardly a vowel sound to it—a word that whispers, breathes out, insinuates itself, but still has a largeness of texture, a surplus of texture in relation to sound. "Ravish" is the perfect word for the end of the poem, embodying as it does a presence, a touch, as well as a violent and threatening kind of intrusion, but an intrusion hollowed out by mystery and distance, an intrusion of the unknown. We can sense where the poem has been if we look at the distance between "batter" and "ravish." By the time we get to "ravish," the explosions in the words have all been internalized and the edges bludgeoned away, leaving a hoarse, insistent sound in the air. This sound is threatening as well, since without the sharpness of "batter" it becomes difficult to locate in space and seems to be coming from everywhere at once.

"Ravish" gives the freedom of the couplet its anxiety. With the couplet, the poem has become a sonnet and is floating free, but uneasily. The couplet stops the forward momentum of the poem with its cross-parallels, which gather the final line back up into the poem rather than propel it ahead. It's as if the poem has been pulled out of time; and to be pulled out of time—to draw time into a kind of spacial clearing—is to wait. In the midst of that clearing, the word "ravish" echoes continuously. It is the *mode* of waiting the poem has chosen. The poem is gathered up like a glass filled to the brim, waiting for someone thirsty to drink it. All this tells us that the poem doesn't exist for its own sake. It is a preparation, an opening out onto a larger mystery and experience.

This experience can only be sketched here, since it is not

something that can ever be talked about. This is the insight of
the poem: not to talk about this experience, but to bring us to
the brink of it. This experience involves the body of the poem,
which is also the body of the poet, John Donne. These two
bodies are one and not one, a relationship that Donne himself
described in a verse-letter, "To Mr. R.W.":

> As this letter is like me, for it
> Hath my name, words, hand, feet, heart, minde and wit

That is, they are one and not one in the same way that Donne is
both identical to and separated from his name etched in the
window, or, on a larger scale, in the same way man's body in
the seventeenth century was identical to and separated from the
body politic and the world's body. In the poem, Donne's body
takes a certain stance, a certain position. He is making a request
of God. In order to make this request, he kneels, and speaks:

> Batter my heart, three person'd God

But what kind of request is this? It is more like a demand.
Imagine Donne kneeling before God, like a suitor before the
king. He kneels to express his humility, his closeness to earth.
In kneeling, the body is off-balance, unprotected, opened
across the front. Kneeling also cuts the body off from its mobility; yet the body is constantly leaning forward, trying to direct
its attention forward. Kneeling is a kind of inward spiral of the
body; the body leans forward and yet holds back, tries to speak
and tries to listen, to be small and to be noticed, to win God's
attention and to yield to him. All these accumulate and build up
and add to the tension as well as the frustration and humility of
kneeling. The poem expresses these tensions perfectly. The
poem also expresses the temptation to spring forward and im-
plore, especially if one's need is great enough:

> Batter my heart, three person'd God; for, you
> As yet but knocke, breathe, shine, and seeke to mend;

That I may rise, and stand, o'erthrow mee,'and bend
Your force, to breake, blowe, burn and make mee new.

Donne is in the position of a suitor who, come to beg a favor of
the king, loses patience and commits the unforgiveable,
by rushing forward off his knees to buttonhole him. This is
why Donne must submit and become passive at the end. Yet
even his submission is in the form of a demand. He asks God to
overthrow him so he may rise and stand, but at the same time
he is in fact rising and standing, precisely so that God will
overthrow him. He cajoles God, orders him, and wants at the
same time to be completely rescued and taken by him, to be
destroyed and made new again. He resents God's distance and
wants him to be close, but he fears that closeness too, and is
unable to open up to it. He can't take a step forward without
God's permission, but he can't get that permission without
approaching God. So he boldly stands up and begins demand-
ing. But he realizes at once that he has done the wrong thing,
and he launches into a hasty explanation:

> I, like an usurpt towne, to'another due,
> Labour to'admit you, but Oh, to no end,
> Reason your viceroy in mee, mee should defend,
> But is captiv'd, and proves weake or untrue,
> Yet dearely'I love you, and would be loved faine,
> But am betroth'd unto your enemie

Finally, Donne is reduced to kneeling again; but he doesn't stop
making demands. However, now the demands are both more
urgent and less astringent. In the lines beginning "Divorce
mee,'untie . . . ," the imperative verbs come first and remain
foremost, and the cadence they establish is almost majestic in
its desire. I sense in these lines a new self-assurance in the
poem, as if Donne knew that his desire, embodied in words,
had been powerful enough to deserve being reciprocated. But
this is something we can never be sure of. The poem doesn't try
to tell us everything; instead, it brings us through what can be

said to the verge of what can't be said. If we speak the poem with our bodies, it leaves us with a shaped bodily stance, the same one the poet assumes by means of the body of the poem. This stance is the hopeful, painful, anxious one of waiting:

> Divorce mee,'untie, or breake that knot againe,
> Take me to you, imprison mee, for I
> Except you'enthrall mee, never shall be free,
> Nor ever chast, except you ravish mee.

TWO

Blake's "The Tyger"

SPEECH FOR Blake was a form of attack. It was a thing in itself, a tool, like the engraver's stylus. It had a shaping power; with it, he could carve things, etch them, make things speak for him, give them, in his phrase, "minute particulars." Speech, in other words, was closely involved with the physical act of writing, and for Blake as an engraver, writing was literally a kind of carving. Blake's etchings of his poems strike me as similar to Chinese calligraphy, in the sense that they embody and express (rather than refuse) the gestures of his own body. For us, typeset letters are an impersonal medium, a kind of no man's land that the author and reader approach from opposite ends. For Blake, writing was not hardened language; it was, on the contrary, language in its most plastic form, language everywhere made supple and expressive by speech. His writing is a score (as in a musical score), but also more than a score. Although I want to talk about "The Tyger" as an auditory experience, a vocal act, I can't ignore the fact that this vocal act is imbedded in a physical form eaten out of copper by acid and then impressed on paper and colored by hand.

In fact, I can't separate the aggressive shaping power of this form from the aggressive shaping power of the sounds it expresses and embodies. In both cases, speech wrestles with the intransigence and resistance of physical things with a brash, unequivocal and direct energy. In the world around him in 1792 Blake had plenty of examples of this kind of energy: the American Revolution, the French Revolution. In his own life and in that of the world, there was an exhilarating kind of will, freedom, energy welling up from within old forms, an energy often symbolized by Blake as hammer-wielding Los, who some critics say framed the tyger's "fearful symmetry." Of course, all the forging, shaping, and twisting in the poem is as much a reflection of Blake's own shaping and etching of copper as it is a reference to his mythological system. And this forging, shaping, and twisting is embedded as well in the movement of the words when we read them:

> Tyger! Tyger! burning bright
> In the forests of the night,
> What immortal hand or eye
> Could frame thy fearful symmetry?
>
> In what distant deeps or skies
> Burnt the fire of thine eyes?
> On what wings dare he aspire?
> What the hand dare seize the fire?

This is a martial cadence. Blake's words advance like a people's army, directly, spontaneously, simply, like the citizens who marched on the Bastille. The words are useful, common, bright Anglo-Saxon words; they were no doubt insults to the specialized, arcane diction that had dominated poetry in the eighteenth century. We feel them as a challenge—they begin by shouting:

> Tyger! Tyger! burning bright
> In the forests of the night,

What immortal hand or eye
Could frame thy fearful symmetry?

In what distant deeps or skies
Burnt the fire of thine eyes?
On what wings dare he aspire?
What the hand dare seize the fire?

And what shoulder, & what art,
Could twist the sinews of thy heart?
And when thy heart began to beat,
What dread hand? & what dread feet?

What the hammer? what the chain?
In what furnace was thy brain?
What the anvil? what dread grasp
Dare its deadly terrors clasp?

All the verbs are active, and all the actions are of seizing,
clasping, twisting, grasping, burning. The world these words
inhabit is almost exclusively one of touch. Furthermore, it's a
world caught in a violent storm, in which a touch immediately
becomes a blow. We *feel* things in this poem, as well as see or
hear them. Blake wants us to imagine not only the tyger's
appearance, but his substance and volume. To give him depth
and weight, he talks about his heart, which burns in the tyger's
innards just as brightly as the tyger himself burns in the forests
of the night.

Actually, this double frame—the heart in the tyger, the tyger
in the night—emphasizes a stillness that the tyger also possesses. Everything is moving, twisting in the poem, and yet
everything is still. Blake has almost trapped his figure in a rigid
outline, in the same way he does the figures in his engravings.
"The great and golden rule of art as well as of life, is this," he
says: "that the more distinct, sharp, and wiry the bounding
line, the more perfect the work of art." In his prints and
watercolors, Blake's aesthetic problem was usually to keep a
strong outline, and yet at the same time burst it in such a way

that the figure inside could gesture beyond itself. In some of the etchings for the Book of Job, he achieves a feeling of liberation by having Satan swoop down in a kind of curved diagonal that ruptures the square space of the border. In the etching called "Glad Day," the figure pushes out against the edge of the paper with his arms, while his torso lifts forward, as if off the page itself.

In "The Tyger," Blake achieves this same kind of explosive liberation of an essentially static figure in a number of ways. First, he uses strong, aggressive, active verbs. Second, he doesn't so much make the tyger move as carefully control our perception of him, to give the impression that he's moving. Throughout the poem, Blake mentions only certain parts of the tyger in order to emphasize the fact that we only partially see it, as we partially see a mountain. First, he gives us a medium close-up; the tyger is in a forest. Then, suddenly, we are inside the tyger, in with the heart, sinews, and brain. Finally, Blake pulls us out, places the tyger in another frame beside a lamb, and repeats the first stanza of the poem, as if to close the outline for good:

> When the stars threw down their spears,
> And water'd heaven with their tears,
> Did he smile his work to see?
> Did he who made the Lamb make thee?
>
> Tyger! Tyger! burning bright
> In the forests of the night,
> What immortal hand or eye
> Dare frame thy fearful symmetry?

He has closed the poem, but it's not really closed. In its center is the tyger, the source of energy for the poem, burning up the outlines that form around him as soon as they form.

The auditory parallel of a firm outline is a firm meter. I've often fantasized the cheering section at a football game chanting the opening stanza of "The Tyger," with a kind of siss-boom-bah build-up, slow and almost whispered at the beginning, but louder and faster with each succeeding line. The trochaic rhythm and the end-stopped lines have that kind of mass self-hypnotized discipline to them, like an army on the march. The rhythm somewhat resembles a heart beat, but it also resembles a measured hammering, or the beating of a drum. For this reason, the poem doesn't accumulate or build, as Donne's "Batter my heart" sonnet does; rather, it begins at a crest, a peak, and remains there. The effect is to make the tyger unequivocal and self-sufficient, having an existence that refuses to *seem*. The spelling of "tyger," incidentally, reinforces this effect. In Blakes' calligraphy, the slant of the "y" is emphasized; or, perhaps we simply feel that it's emphasized because we aren't used to seeing it there. At any rate, the effect is somewhat like giving an Englishman Oriental cheek bones and eyes: we *know* we're in the presence of an unusual and striking creature. We also know that we're in foreign territory, without the usual rules (including rules of spelling) to guide us.

So the poem has a rigid outline; we feel it as we read, in the meter and in the repetition of the opening stanza at the end. Speech in the poem has the effect of something carved or etched in a medium that will keep its shape sharply and firmly and will hold in all the potential explosions of the active verbs and the rapidly shifting perspective. However, it can't hold everything in. The poem also employs one more device of great simplicity that enables it to continually burst through its rigid outline. I am thinking of the fact that every sentence in the poem exists as a question. I think this may be because Blake sensed the resistance of the world to his language and the resistance of the tyger to be named, or even to be talked about. A question is a refusal to place limits on something. It stakes out a realm, but opens (rather than closes) possibilities in that realm. It refuses to package, nail down, or conclude. A question is a way of designating something while setting it free, a form of naming in which the name has no power of its own, but humbles itself before the thing. Good questions are also thoughtful, but they are thought existing as an act, a process, rather than an already digested set of conclusions. "Thought is Act," Blake said, and he also said, "As the true method of knowledge is experiment, the true faculty of knowing must be the faculty which experiences." Questions are knowledge as experience, as well as perceptions that actively rather than passively encounter the world.

Questions are also, strangely, both a tactful and desperate form of speech, appropriate for a reality sufficiently large and mysterious enough to scare us. In Blake's poem, questions are the slits through which he shows us that reality and gives us some idea of its dimensions. The effect is similar to one of his Proverbs of Hell: "The roaring of lions, the howling of wolves, the raging of the stormy sea, and the destructive sword, are portions of eternity, too great for the eye of man." The wonderful thing about the poem is that through the form of questions, the tyger is both revealed and not revealed. He shines forth with a firm outline, and yet his mystery is preserved. This is because it is the mystery itself that shines forth, the unnamability that is named:

> Tyger! Tyger! burning bright
> In the forests of the night,
> What immortal hand or eye
> Could frame thy fearful symmetry?
>
> In what distant deeps or skies
> Burnt the fire of thine eyes?
> On what wings does he aspire?
> What the hand dare seize the fire?

The tyger is mysterious, but his mystery has weight and substance. At the heart of their uncertainty and awe, the questions contain a residue of materiality; out of this residue, the tyger constructs a body. This is simply to say that when the questions ask who twisted the sinews of the tyger's heart, or who forged his brain, that heart and that brain are residues of those questions, and they help to create the tyger's body:

> And what shoulder, & what art,
> Could twist the sinews of thy heart?
> And when thy heart began to beat,
> What dread hand? & what dread feet?
>
> What the hammer? what the chain?
> In what furnace was thy brain?
> What the anvil? what dread grasp
> Dare its deadly terrors clasp?

The questions are the substance of the poem, in the sense that they are the chief form speech takes. But they are a kind of insubstantial substance, in that they literally unfulfill the poem, open up the mouth of speech in the poem. The questions serve to underline the fact that the poem is both a thing and an act, both matter and energy. In this sense, the words of the poem are indistinguishable from their subject matter. Like the poem, the tyger is both matter and energy; its body is open, like the body of fire, a kind of matter that leaps out of itself, in a perpetual state of transformation.

The final two stanzas close the body that has been born, give it the outline and weight it needs in order to have autonomy and freedom. At the same time, the body is still bursting outward, still being born, or still escaping itself:

> When the stars threw down their spears,
> And water'd heaven with their tears.
> Did he smile his work to see?
> Did he who made the Lamb make thee?

> Tyger! Tyger! burning bright
> In the forests of the night,
> What immortal hand or eye
> Dare frame thy fearful symmetry?

Blake's firm outline that refuses to confine shows us that a body is never an accomplished thing, but a series of transformations. I am talking now about both the body of the tyger and the body of the poem: in the last analysis, they are the same. To exist, a body needs to be in a permanent open-closed state. In *The Book of Urizen,* when Orc is born, a girdle grows around his chest, which he breaks, then another girdle grows, which he breaks, and so forth—"The girdle was form'd by day,/ By night was burst in twain." Existence for Blake is always just coming into existence. This is why energy is so important for him. Existence is never passive but active, because it is continually reborn. The tyger fully exists when the poem begins—"Tyger! Tyger! burning bright"—but it is also just coming into existence. The best image of this is fire: a crest held but breaking out of itself, a body perpetually present and perpetually born.

THREE

A Sonnet by Mallarmé

MALLARMÉ SHOWS US what happens when that intransigent world Blake tried to shape ceases to exist and language takes its place as the Other, the subject matter and the substance that the poem *approaches* as well as speaks. Mallarmé's work is the product of a culture entirely different from Donne's or Blake's, a culture for which language was becoming hardened, objectified and fragmented, and words and things were becoming separated from each other. A case could be made for Mallarmé's genius, in fact, solely on the basis that he was the first to perceive this and make adjustments in his poetry. Actually, however, other poets made adjustments too, but very different ones; Whitman, in particular, adjusted in the very opposite direction, as we'll see.

For Mallarmé, language is closed off from the body and from the world. Mallarmé confirms the structuralist view that language is diacritical and that words refer only to other words. In fact, along with de Saussure, Mallarmé looms as one of the great influences upon structuralist thought. Michel Foucault says (in *The Order of Things*) that gradually in the nineteenth century, language came to be thought of as something not transparent, but as a substance with an interior space and anatomy of its own. With this view of language, *literature* as such came into existence. Mallarmé didn't invent simply modern literature, but (possibly along with Flaubert), literature itself, literature as a pure, separate language, stripped of the necessity of representation, reduced simply to the act of writing. Foucault doesn't emphasize the word "writing," but I'm sure he understands its implications. A poem for Mallarmé is not an act of speech, but of writing. "Everything in the world," he said, "exists to end in a book." Or, to put it another way, the less tightly woven into the world one's poems are, the more tightly woven into language they will be. Since it is a reciprocal act, speech is inappropriate for an attitude that regards the earth, experience, matter, as poor meager things compared to the sublime richness of words; much more appropriate is the act of writing, which is capable of pulling language like a cloak around itself. This is an act of writing entirely different from Blake's etchings, which attempt to carve and shape things, and which by extension wrestle with the resistances of the world. In Mallarmé, writing wrestles with, carves and shapes, only itself. His language doesn't copy or report or represent an already existing world, but creates a world, a purely linguistic world. Actually, no poetry simply represents a world, not even the most seemingly transparent poetry, such as Whitman's. All words, in fact, contain both a reference to other words and a reference to things. Mallarmé couldn't entirely erase the world from his poems, just as Whitman couldn't simply represent it. But what Mallarmé could do is reverse the normal relationship between word and thing, so that rather than the poem existing for the sake of the subject matter, the subject matter exists for the sake of the poem. Another way of putting this is to say that while all poetry uses words to call things forward, that is, lodges the word in the thing, Mallarmé also reverses this process and lodges the thing in the word, so that the word itself becomes a thing. This thing the word becomes is language.

In the sonnet beginning "Dame, sans trop d'ardeur . . . ," there is a woman present in a room; by implication, the speaker of the poem is also present. There are also certain domestic objects, articles of clothing, a rose, jewelry, a fan. But when we read the poem, we are not aware of these bodies or things as physical beings. As Wallace Fowlie says, Mallarmé's poems are a kind of chemical solution that he throws on things in order to make them dissolve. What we are aware of is words and the strange relationships between them:

> Dame
>
> > sans trop d'ardeur à la fois enflammant
> La rose qui cruelle ou déchirée et lasse
> Même du blanc habit de pourpre le délace
> Pour ouïr dans sa chair pleurer le diamant

> [Lady
>
> > without too much warmth at once enflaming
> The rose which cruel or torn and tired
> Even of the white coat with purple unlaces it
> In order to hear in the flesh the weeping diamond]

The first thing we experience, I think, is the confusion of the tangled syntax, as well as the fact that certain words seem to possess a kind of stillness in the midst of that confusion: "Dame," "rose," "habit," "pourpre," "chair," "diamant." The tangled syntax sets these words off as hard, impenetrable, untangled, and, in their isolation, jewellike. The mind perceives words in a poem, Mallarmé says in "Le Mystère Dans Les Lettres," "independently of the ordinary sequence, projected like the walls of a cavern, as long as their mobility or principle lasts, being that part of discourse which is not spoken."[1] In the

<hr>

1. Most of the translations of Mallarmé's prose are taken from *Mallarmé*, ed. Anthony Hartley (Penguin Books, 1965). The translation of the poem is my own.

poem, each word is a kind of cave with its own interior distance that is not absorbed into the process of the poem, into the syntax, since that syntax is at least held in suspense, waiting for more words to complete it, and may even have deliberately mutilated itself in order to direct all our attention to the words it bears up. In other words, the relationship between the words seems to have been sacrificed in favor of the Word in isolation, each separate one a jewel that wants to appropriate all the light and color in the poem for itself alone:

> Dame
> sans trop d'ardeur à la fois enflammant
> La rose qui cruelle ou déchirée et lasse
> Même du blanc habit de pourpre le délace
> Pour ouïr dans sa chair pleurer le diamant
>
> Oui sans ces crises de rosée et gentiment
> Ni brise quoique, avec, le ciel orageux passe
> Jalouse d'apporter je ne sais quel espace
> Au simple jour le jour très vrai du sentiment
>
> [Lady
> without too much warmth at once enflaming
> The rose which cruel or torn and tired
> Even of the white coat with purple unlaces it
> In order to hear in the flesh the weeping diamond
>
> Yes without these crises of dew and nicely
> Nor breeze although, with, the stormy sky passes
> Jealous to bring I don't know what space
> To the simple day after day of sentiment]

In a sense, Mallarmé's language repels things. All we have are words existing in a state of splendid exile. When a jewel is present, everything else is the lack of that jewel. In the same way, as Wallace Fowlie puts it, the word, for Mallarmé, is "the absence of the thing it designates." Words are like Hérodiade in Mallarmé's longest poem: too proud and beautiful to be touched by people or by things.

For this reason, language in Mallarmé has lost its power to name; or rather, language names only itself. Things are conjured rather than named and made present; we have their resonance, taste, or memory. For Mallarmé, the absence of something is more evocative than its presence. At the end of "Surgi de la Croupe," a vase imagines the rose it could be holding. As Fowlie points out, Mallarmé's work dwells repeatedly on empty things, shells of things: an empty jar of rouge against a wall (representing the poet's exhausted mind), an empty helmet, a mirror, a window, a conch shell, an empty tomb. This emptiness or lack has two faces in Mallarmé. On the one hand it represents a kind of impotence, especially an impotence of language, which is powerless to call forth or open onto things. On the other hand, it accounts for the suggestiveness and mystery in Mallarmé, which is his true power. His poems are like precious objects which refuse to disclose themselves, which will always remain essentially unopened. "Every holy thing wishing to remain holy surrounds itself with mystery," he said. Still, this mystery is obtained at the cost of severing language from things. Mallarmé drives language into itself like a wedge in order to give it the weight it has abandoned in abandoning the world. Each word has the weight not only of itself, but of all the other words—not things—it refers to. As we read a poem by Mallarmé, each word becomes the apex of a pyramid that all the other words are struggling to achieve.

This struggle of words to dominate the poem couldn't take place without involving grammar and syntax. In all of Mallarmé's poems there is a battle between the sovereign word on the one hand and grammar and syntax on the other. The word is never the tip of a lash in Mallarmé (as it is in Whitman), never the result of a force or desire that comes from outside of itself. The word is sovereign and tries to keep in check any process or desire that threatens to swell up around it. Around the word,

the syntax is a kind of mindless mass of tangled roots, turning
in on itself or opening onto nothing; or at least, that's what it
appears to be at first:

Dame
        sans trop d'ardeur à la fois enflammant
La rose qui cruelle ou déchirée et lasse
Même du blanc habit de pourpre le délace
Pour ouïr dans sa chair pleurer le diamant

Oui sans ces crises de rosée et gentiment
Ni brise quoique, avec, le ciel orageux passe
Jalouse d'apporter je ne sais quel espace
Au simple jour le jour très vrai du sentiment

[Lady
        without too much warmth at once enflaming
The rose which cruel or torn and tired
Even of the white coat with purple unlaces it
In order to hear in the flesh the weeping diamant

Yes without these crises of dew and nicely
Nor breeze although, with, the stormy sky passes
Jealous to bring I don't know what space
To the simple day after day of sentiment]

At this point in the poem, one brief statement has emerged (La
rose le délace), but has immediately been swallowed into the
ongoing incompletion of the syntax, like a shooting star that
flared up and died out the next instant. Overall, the syntax is
still in a state of suspension. We still haven't come to the main
subject, verb, and predicate. Mallarmé loves inversions, loves
to begin a statement with prepositional phrases, as he does
here, and to withhold completion of the statement for as long as
he can. In one poem, he talks about a tomb which "Hélas! du
manque seul des lourds bouquets s'encombre" [Alas! of the
lack only of heavy bouquets encumbers itself]. This kind of
language, rather than uncoiling or unfolding, coils up, gathers
into itself. The initial words lack the remaining words not as
something that will complete them but as something that they

(the initial words) will complete. The effect is to make the line disappear into itself, like a snake swallowing its tail. In this particular line, the effect is appropriate, since the words describe something that doesn't exist: heavy flowers whose lack encumbers a tomb. But the effect would be appropriate in almost any poem, since Mallarmé's words are always the absence rather than the presence of a thing. Actually, the line doesn't disappear into itself as much as it does into those words, giving them all of the authority of the poem. The syntax is a means by which the poem drains into the loneliness of each separate word, and by which each separate word thus becomes released from the syntax, and, as a result, from time.

Yet, at the same time, Mallarmé's inversions and periodic sentences have the opposite effect: they drive the poem into time, by giving it a forward momentum. When the principal elements of a phrase are withheld, the syntax continually needs completion, and we are impelled forward in search of it. In the sonnet "A la nue accablante tu," the subject of the one sentence in the poem occurs in line 5, and the principal verb in line 8. In reading the opening lines we naturally wonder what is "a la nue accablante tu" (under the massive cloud silenced). So a kind of suspense is created, and a tension in the language that keeps us moving through it. Yet, once we know what is silenced under that cloud (a shipwreck) and what that shipwreck does (abolishes the mast), then this tension is neutralized. Then we have to go back against the current of the language, and reorder our impressions of the initial lines, since now we know what they referred to. Almost all of Mallarmé's poems have this forward and backward movement, which occurs on a small scale in the line and on a large scale in the poem as a whole. We are carried forward by withheld information and then must struggle backward in order to plug that information into what we've already read.

In this respect, the syntax is not entirely mindless. It is, as

Jacques Derrida points out (in *La Dissémination*), an ingenious machine, a complex game. It exists in a very shady realm—one which we know almost nothing about—between the mechanical and the organic. It is mechanical because it has been carefully blueprinted, pieced together with ingenious and painstaking patience. But it is organic because it seems to have a will of its own and is capable of spontaneously generating new shoots and branches at almost any moment. This most frightening and startling feature of the syntax lies at the node of the curious relationship between syntax and word. The word exists caught in the net of that syntax, like a rat in a maze, trying to find its way out; the word exists for the sake of the syntax. And yet, the syntax exists in order to free the word of its normal responsibilities; that is, the syntax violates and cripples itself, disregards all the rules that usually make it possible, in order to allow the word to assert its autonomy and independence. The syntax is a game that a few words win. It traps the word in its ingenious labyrinth, but to be trapped is to experience the first taste of freedom, which the word then triumphantly achieves. The syntax is potential, and the word is achievement. For example, any noun can become the subject of a new sentence or clause, regardless of what function or position it already occupies. In the first stanza of the poem, phrases, clauses, and even a sentence spin off the word "rose" in all directions, like formless moons from a young planet. Meanwhile, the prime mover of all this activity, "rose," remains aloof from it at the same time, as if it created the activity absentmindedly out of the excess of its self-reliance. In the second stanza, this fluidity of syntax has reached almost the state of chaos; an adverb (*gentiment*) has appeared where one expects a noun, and a negation has been cut in half. At the same time, the prepositional phrase in which these occur, the phrase that began with the impetus of being the opening of a stanza and a parallel to the opening of

the poem—a kind of second beginning—only to find itself
crumbling, as if syntax itself had decided to abandon it—this
entire phrase is called back just as it passes by, called back and
turned around by one word, "avec," so that it seems to both
double itself and disappear at the same time:

> Oui sans ces crises de rosée et gentiment
> Ni brise quoique, avec, le ciel orageux passe
>
> [Yes without these crises of dew and nicely
> Nor breeze although, with, the stormy sky passes]

In the battle between sovereign word and syntax, certain key
words usually emerge as triumphant, in this case "rose" and
"avec." Many words are simply buried by or submerged in the
syntax; but these two in particular become walls before which
phrases and clauses suddenly halt or dissolve, as well as sources
of new phrases and clauses.

Around these words, the syntax twists like an arabesque.
Phrases and clauses are truncated, incompletions and inversions overlap, asides become the main thought, and all of this
density suddenly opens out onto a simple declarative statement. When this arabesque begins to spill out of itself, like the
innards of a strange animal, then it becomes apparent that only
the poet's will can hold it all together, let alone extract something out of it. Mallarmé may have wanted, as he said in "Crise
de Vers," to "yield the initiative to words," but this only made
it all the more necessary to impose his will on the poem, since
words, by themselves, are unruly things. At times, reading
Mallarmé is a kind of amnesia, in which not only previous
statements, but previous parts of statements, previous phrases,
the part of *this* phrase just read, are forgotten, slip out of mind,
can't be held, and cease to have any effect on what comes after
them, so that anything, it seems, could come next. At first
reading, it always seems that nothing could be more chaotic

than this, as if the syntax had the widest possible view of the
way ahead and no view at all of the way behind. Yet, we
generally discover that something, finally, does emerge. The
initiative is yielded to words, but only in such a way that, as
Mallarmé also said, "Chance does not touch a line of verse, that
is the great thing." This contradiction is a tightrope that all of
Mallarmé's poems walk. Out of the plethora of possibilities in
the syntax, out of all the cul-de-sacs, detours, circular passages,
and doors that open out onto nothing, a grammar as we know
it, even a sentence, does emerge, subtle but firm, like an
exhausted explorer out of a jungle:

> Dame
>   sans trop d'ardeur à la fois enflammant
> La rose qui cruelle ou déchirée et lasse
> Même du blanc habit de pourpre le délace
> Pour ouïr dans sa chair pleurer le diamant
>
> Oui sans ces crises de rosée et gentiment
> Ni brise quoique, avec, le ciel orageux passe
> Jalouse d'apporter je ne sais quel espace
> Au simple jour le jour très vrai du sentiment
>
> Ne te semble-t-il pas, disons, que chaque année
> Dont sur ton front renaît la grâce spontanée
> Suffise selon quelque apparence et pour moi
>
> [Lady
>   without too much warmth at once enflaming
> The rose which cruel or torn and tired
> Even of the white coat with purple unlaces it
> In order to hear in the flesh the weeping diamond
>
> Yes without these crises of dew and nicely
> Nor breeze although, with, the stormy sky passes
> Jealous to bring I don't know what space
> To the simple day after day of sentiment
>
> Does it not seem to you, let us say, that each year
> Of which on your brow the spontaneous grace is reborn
> Suffices according to some appearance and for me]

But once again, this sentence, the second one in the poem, disappears almost as soon as it appears: "ne te semble-t-il pas" [does it not seem to you]. Even more than the first (*la rose le delace*), this sentence is a weak, fragile, fading thing, almost a ghost. At its heart, it is practically an absence, like most of Mallarmé's poems are at their hearts. Not only does it deal with seeming rather than being, but it is a question and a negation at the same time. Still, it does the job. What seemed completely random in the second stanza has had a kind of necessity conferred on it in retrospect. But we have to go back, at least in our imaginations, in order to experience that necessity, and once again the process by which the syntax unfolds has abolished itself. Meanwhile, the rest of the poem, the final tercet, is dropping like a plum out of the completion of the syntax, a fruit of the marriage of the poem to itself:

> Comme un éventail frais dans la chambre s'étonne
> À raviver du peu qu'il faut ici d'émoi
> Toute notre native amitié monotone.

> [As a cool fan in the room wonders
> At what little emotion it takes to revive
> Our whole friendship natural and monotonous.]

At the end, the poem seems not only exhausted, but a little bored too. The monotony mentioned in the last line is almost an answer to our uneasy feeling when we were lost in the syntax and wondered if anything would be completed. All this time, the poet has been reclining on his couch, languid, but confident that his poem will achieve itself, that the skin of the poem will be filled out, although certainly without bursting. However, if we look closely we can see the beads of sweat on his neck. The poem has achieved itself, but at the cost of a tremendous effort of the will. But Mallarmé doesn't want this effort to show. At the end, he wants the poem to be released from all effort, all process, all exertion. This is why he's held the poem in check so carefully: so that it wouldn't accumulate, wouldn't repeat itself and build in intensity by means of a rhythm, wouldn't become a process, a flood. The poem is a space in which to insert words, as a jeweler inserts diamonds on a brooch. Words don't arise out of the accumulated pressure of previous words or out of the rhythm of words. A word may appear because of its relation to words yet to come. So in a sense, those words yet to come already exist; the poet leaves nothing to chance. The continual aim of the process of composition in Mallarmé is to abolish process, as it is in Poe's "Philosophy of Composition," which Mallarmé knew and admired. This is because Mallarmé wanted to free the poem from circumstance, matter, time, and chance. He wanted his poems to be written, not spoken, since the human voice is dominated by the body, which itself is dominated by time and matter. And once written, he wanted his poems to be closed up in a book. The image of a closed book held a fascination for Mallarmé. In the sonnet "Mes bouquins refermés sur le nom de Paphos" [My books closed on the name of Paphos], the closed book represents imagination itself, which shuts out the world and exists for its own sake.

Yet, for all this, the world could never be completely shut out. Matter, process, things, and even the body, do participate in Mallarmé's poetry. Mallarmé's poems all represent a kind of triumph over matter; but as soon as the triumph is achieved, matter begins to leak up again along the edges and into the cracks of the poem. Mallarmé realized this. At the end of "Prose Pour des Esseintes," the word carved in the tomb, "Pulchérie" [beauty], is "Caché par le trop grand glaïeul" [hidden by the too large gladiolas]. I take this to mean that the world whose reality is continually called into doubt in the poem is real enough at the end to obscure language and its disembodied beauty. As much as he wanted it to be, language couldn't be the only reality for Mallarmé. This is because words, no matter how disembodied, always have a residue of materiality; either they have a sensual sound or texture, or they still possess an echo of the thing they represent. In "Dame, sans trop d'ardeur . . . ," the rose, flesh, the diamond are certainly unreal; we don't sense an actual rose or actual flesh. Their reality is almost entirely linguistic. Still, there is a kind of leftover sensuality they create, which hovers threateningly around the edges of the poem, along with the dew, storms, crises, the not *too* much warmth that enflames. These create a cloud of sensual materiality that threatens the languid, passive, monotonous existence of the speaker and his lady, a cloud that they have waved off with surprisingly little emotion, but whose existence they can't help but be aware of. In fact, this is probably the "point" of the poem, to the extent that it has one.

Furthermore, this point is made entirely by nuance and suggestion, never by statement. As Mallarmé said, he wanted his words to light each other up by mutual reflection. I take this to mean that he wanted to release the gestural significance of words: not their dictionary meanings, but the *play* of meanings among them. This is difficult to do when each word is also sculpted, pure, and isolated. But in fact, when words are so sovereign, perhaps that's all that's left for them to do: to create a tone, a nuance, a kind of afterglow. In this sense, Mallarmé's poetry is perhaps supremely a poetry of the body; he drives the suggestive gestures of the body into, not the words, but the spaces between the words, so that what counts is never denotation but connotation, never statement but atmosphere. However, Mallarmé's poetry at the same time holds back from the weight and energy of the body, and from the breathlessness, expansiveness, and desire of speech. So it is a kind of poetry of the body without the body, a poetry of curiously disembodied gestures.

We can see this too if we think of Mallarmé's attempt to

neutralize process in his poems. By turning the syntax back on itself and releasing the words from time, he hollows out the actual act of composition, and by extension, the act of reading. Normally, this act is purely successive, and exists in time and process; it is process itself. But Mallarmé wants to freeze process; ideally, a poem should be apprehended in one moment, as one word. But this is impossible, and process creeps in, finally, to unfold the poem. In "Dame sans trop d'ardeur," this process is the emergence of the second sentence out of the forest of tangled syntax in the poem. Even though the sentence sends us back into the poem to reorder our impressions of what came before it, still, at the same time, it has emerged from the poem, and emerged against considerable resistance. There's no doubt that from the involuted labyrinth of the second quatrain to the relative calm and repose of the first tercet, there is a progression, an achievement, because an actual sentence takes shape. Shape emerges out of shapelessness. In the case of both Donne and Blake, we saw how a poem is both a thing and an act. In the case of Mallarmé, we see how the poem wants to be a thing, but can't help but be an act too:

Dame
        sans trop d'ardeur à la fois enflammant
La rose qui cruelle ou déchirée et lasse
Même du blanc habit de pourpre le délace
Pour ouïr dans sa chair pleurer le diamant

Oui sans ces crises de rosée et gentiment
Ni brise quoique, avec, le ciel orageux passe
Jalouse d'apporter je ne sais quel espace
Au simple jour le jour très vrai du sentiment

Ne te semble-t-il pas, disons, que chaque année
Dont sur ton front renaît la grâce spontanée
Suffise selon quelque apparence et pour moi

Comme un éventail frais dans la chambre s'étonne
À raviver du peu qu'il faut ici d'émoi
Toute notre native amitié monotone.

[Lady
            without too much warmth at one enflaming
The rose which cruel or torn and tired
Even of the white coat with purple unlaces it
In order to hear in the flesh the weeping diamond

Yes without these crises of dew and nicely
Nor breeze although, with, the stormy sky passes
Jealous to bring I don't know what space
To the simple day after day of sentiment

Does it not seem to you, let us say, that each year
Of which on your brow the spontaneous grace is reborn
Suffices according to some appearance and for me

As a cool fan in the room wonders
At what little emotion it takes to revive
Our whole friendship natural and monotonous.]

Finally, we are left with a sense of Mallarmé's poem as a body, but a body whose existence is extremely fleeting and contingent. Hardly is it born before it disappears, and leaves only an afterimage behind. This is the price Mallarmé paid for trying to create a world without process (and why he had such difficulty in writing long poems). Time became serial for him, fragmented, like the jewellike words in his poems. The poet's body leapt out of itself briefly, and then almost immediately pulled itself down, reminding him of his thingness and mortality. A lifetime became collapsed into these few instants, each time the poet picked up his pen, which is probably why he tried to put everything he knew into each separate poem. In a sense, each poem, in relation to the others, became like the words within it, and sat at the apex of a pyramid which the others were trying to climb

It is as if each one of Mallarmé's poems were trying to come closer to a vanishing point. His body brushed the poem in its struggle to attain that point and even warmed the words a bit before they hardened and became jewels. But finally, even the warmth and grace of the body couldn't prevent that beautiful language from flying into itself.

PART IV Naked Poetry

ONE Naked Poetry

Mallarmé represents the beginning of a long tradition in modern literature, a tradition whose poets have perceived the gap between words and things and between language and speech, and have chosen to dwell in a language which is always referring to itself, which has a weight and opacity that language never had before. Mallarmé, T. S. Eliot, Hart Crane, and James Joyce are probably the masters of this tradition. Language in *Finnegans Wake*, for example, is a labyrinth of languages, a blind internal surface, an almost gothic inner space of massive weight and endless passageways. Still, this tradition represents only one possible adjustment to the hardening of language in modern culture. There's another tradition that made the opposite adjustment. To begin talking about it, I'd like to mention again the spectrum I described in the first chapter, with gestures on one end, language on the other, and speech ranging across the arc in the middle. In the Mallarmé tradition, the weight of speech is given over to language and the interior depths of language. In the other tradition, which probably begins with Whitman, the weight of speech is given over to gestures and the kinetic energy of gestures. Whitman, D. H. Lawrence, Rilke, William Carlos Williams, and a number of Spanish-speaking poets such as Federico García Lorca, César Vallejo, and Pablo Neruda are probably the masters of this tradition. I call it "naked poetry" not because these poets are interested in self-revelation (although a few are), but because of a certain condition of speech in their poetry. Speech for these poets is an energy, a going forth, an opening onto the world, and so a means to an end, not an end in itself. I should mention before going on that the distinction between these traditions isn't absolute. I am talking about broad movements that often recede very rapidly into the background when we are faced with the uniqueness of a particular poet. Some of the best modern poets—Rimbaud, Pound, and Stevens, for example—fit into both groups. Others, like Yeats, fit into neither.

But even if the line between them is sometimes blurred, the main currents of the two traditions are fairly distinct. Today, we can see the second tradition more clearly because it is also the tradition of free verse, which has become a dominant mode of poetry for us. We know free verse by a lot of other names: organic form, temporal form, expressive form, open form. In free verse, the form doesn't exist as clothing, that is, doesn't exist prior to the poem. In clothed or formal verse, the prior existence of form means that the poem often becomes stylized, like clothing that must obey a certain fashion; and the poet is consequently tempted to rely on ornament or rhetoric. Of course, free verse doesn't guarantee that this temptation will be overcome, just as clothed verse doesn't guarantee that it will be succumbed to. Ornament is a danger of clothed verse. The dangers of free verse involve different matters, as we'll see.

The Spanish poet Jiménez talks about this stylization and ornament in the poem from which the phrase "naked poetry" is taken, "At First She Came to Me Pure" (translation by Robert Bly):

At first she came to me pure,
dressed only in her innocence;
and I loved her as we love a child.

Then she began putting on
clothes she picked up somewhere;
and I hated her, without knowing it.

She gradually became a queen,
the jewelry was blinding . . .
What bitterness and rage!

She started going back toward nakedness.
And I smiled.

Soon she was back to the single shift
of her old innocence.
I believed in her a second time.

Then she took off the cloth
and was entirely naked . . .
naked poetry, always mine,
that I have loved my whole life!

Jiménez shows that naked poetry is poetry in which language is
no longer a dress or veil. Whitman uses a similar metaphor in
the 1855 preface to *Leaves of Grass:* "I will not have in my
writing any elegance or effect or originality to hang in the way
between me and the rest like curtains," he says. "I will have
nothing hang in the way, not the richest curtains." This was an
unusual standard for poetry in Whitman's time, but one that
has won wide favor today. Poetry has come to be accepted not
solely as a craft or discipline, and not as an elegant, clever, or
even beautiful use of words, but rather as an extension of
consciousness, even of the writer's personality. Obviously,
such a standard raises questions and entails dangers, the most
pressing having to do with form. The assumption seems to be
that naked poets can dispense with form if their personality is
strong enough. Whitman is probably the source of this assumption, having called *Leaves of Grass* "an attempt, from first to last,
to put a *Person,* a human being (myself in the latter half of the

Nineteenth Century, in America) freely, fully, and truly on record." He succeeded in the attempt, but not by dispensing with form. Still, the form involved himself, his own personality, his own body, much more intimately than any of the traditional poetic forms. Diane Wakoski calls this form one in which "the naked form is the poet himself."

When the poet speaks from his own person, the form is not clothing or a mask, but a presence in the world itself, a voice, a mouth, a body. It has to be open to sudden changes, to quirky spontaneous things happening, to the fluid, the individual, and the private. This is why naked poetry so often occurs in the present tense. D. H. Lawrence calls free verse "the unrestful, ungraspable poetry of the sheer present, poetry whose very permanency lies in its wind-like transit." Naked poetry is the kind of poetry written when the past has ceased to exist, or at least has ceased to be a satisfying measure of the present. The danger of this kind of poetry is that when poets move out into the unknown, there are no rules or guidelines; they can't take refuge in the past. So the poem proceeds through the doubts and hesitations of the present moment, through trial and error, as many of Lawrence's poems do. Form in this kind of poetry is a bodily activity similar to the description of walking Williams quotes in *Paterson*, from an essay originally in the *Journal of the American Medical Association*: "The good walker should be able to change pace, stop, start, turn, step up or down, twist or stoop, easily and quickly, without losing balance or rhythm." If, as Valéry says, poetry is like dancing and prose is like walking, then naked poetry, halfway between poetry and prose, is like walking that has been transformed into a dance, while still retaining the character of walking.

One poet who loved to walk was Whitman. The long, loping gait of his line is the gait of an insatiable walker. In walking, the landscape opens up for us as the body passes through it. "The earth expanding right hand and left hand," he says in "Song of the Open Road." Many of his most characteristic poems are walking poems. In "There Was a Child Went Forth," the child in the poem walks through the world of things while the world of things at the same time flows through him. Here are the opening stanzas:

> There was a child went forth every day,
> And the first object he look'd upon, that object he became,
> And that object became part of him for the day or a certain part
> of the day,
> Or for many years or stretching cycles of years.
>
> The early lilacs became part of this child,
> And grass and white and red morning-glories, and white and
> red clover, and the song of the phoebe-bird,
> And the Third-month lambs and the sow's pink-faint litter, and
> the mare's foal and the cow's calf,
> And the noisy brood of the barnyard or by the mire of the
> pondside,
> And the fish suspending themselves so curiously below there,
> and the beautiful curious liquid,
> And the water-plants with their graceful flat heads, all became
> part of him.
>
> The field-sprouts of Fourth-month and Fifth-month became
> part of him,
> Winter-grain sprouts and those of the light-yellow corn, and
> the esculent roots of the garden,
> And the apple-trees cover'd with blossoms and the fruit
> afterward, and wood-berries, and the commonest
> weeds by the road,
> And the old drunkard staggering home from the outhouse of
> the tavern whence he had lately risen,
> And the schoolmistress that pass'd on her way to the school,
> And the friendly boys that pass'd, and the quarrelsome boys,
> And the tidy and fresh-cheek'd girls, and the barefoot negro
> boy and girl,
> And all the changes of city and country wherever he went.

The words in this poem don't crowd or outstrip each other. In contrast to Donne, this is not a poetry of desire. It consists of nouns, not verbs. In this poem, Whitman's vision of democracy extends to nature and to language. *Things* in Whitman's world are democratic. There is no intense desire of one thing for another, of fire for the sun, or the soul for God, as there is in Donne's world. Or rather, this desire is democratized, spread out, universalized. Since there is no hierarchy, no Chain of Being, Whitman's world is one of continual release and sympathy, of objects becoming part of other objects, objects becoming part of persons, and of persons uniting through sympathy, with their arms about each other's necks. As he put it in "Song of Myself": "And these one and all tend inward to me, and I tend outward to them."

The same is true of Whitman's language. Words in Whitman are never more comfortable than when they occur in large numbers, when they not only signify the democratic plenitude of the world, but also become part of that plenitude. Whitman's poems are not coiled springs, as Donne's and Mallarmé's are. It rarely happens that any one particular word becomes more important than another. The word in Whitman opens rather than closes the poem. In Mallarmé, the poem backs up or becomes lodged in individual words, but in Whitman, the word is the tip of a lash, the mouth of a river. The word in fact, isn't as important as the energy that gives rise to and passes through words. Often, words tend to dissolve into the line, in the same way letters dissolve into words. In Mallarmé, words speak themselves; but in Whitman, Walt Whitman speaks. He never stops reminding us of this fact. Of course, "Walt Whitman" may very well be a creation of Whitman's poems. But the point is that words in those poems always exist in process and are always an utterance of a person in an actual place and time. This person may very well have shown us himself only as he wanted to be seen, if we think of that sort of thing in terms of autobiography, the content and details of the poems. But if we think of it in terms of an act of speech, then Whitman's poems are totally naked, in the sense that words are a transparent gesture of his body, not things in themselves. "What do you think words are?" he asks in the *American Primer*. "Do you think words are positive and original things in themselves?— No: Words are not original and arbitrary in themselves—Words are a result."

Another way of saying this is that Whitman's poems are usually engaged in an act of discovery. All poems are both open and closed, but Mallarmé's are more closed than open, and Whitman's more open than closed. Robert Bly has described Whitman's poems as tunnels: open to the world at either end. This is true of all naked poems, and has important implications for the form or body these poems take. To be engaged in an act of discovery is in a sense to exist in the transition from a discarded or shapeless world to a new world, one being born. The discarded world is chaotic, raw, uncooked. The new one is in the process of taking on a form or body; it is the poem itself. But these aren't simply two worlds. The formed and the formless are always bleeding into each other. The poem is in fact the act of emerging from the formless into the formed. Often, it slips back into the discarded or formless; often, too, it outstrips itself into the chiseled, the exact. The poem is like a fish emerging from water, a formed thing coming out of the unformed. But its body (like that of the fish) will be appropriate to the unformed, will be an accumulation or summary of forces in it. The unformed is not a backdrop or ideal space. The poem is not a ship, but a fish; it is capable of submerging in the unformed while still retaining its integrity. Its substance is a kind of mesh, woven out of formlessness but slowly discovering the compactness of a body. Still, that compactness is never certain, and the body often becomes limp and boneless. This means, for example, that the poem will occasionally slip into 'mere' speech—like a dance slipping into a walk—and that the psychic energy of the poem will become general and unarticulated, as in surrealism; that is, the poem will slip back into a kind of collective unconscious below the level of personality or formed things, and will proceed through what seem to be accidental verbal conjunctions, words that drift together like logs on a river.

Pablo Neruda's "Sexual Water" is a good example. The entire poem wavers on the edge between order and chaos, the bound and the unbound. Neruda establishes a horizon in the poem sufficiently open for objects to come and go freely, a fluid horizon in which objects can be captured in such a way that they are released at the same time. This horizon is water itself, in which things share a general and unarticulated nature, while they are at the same time things with their own autonomy, buoyed up by water. Here is part of the poem (translated by Robert Bly):

> It is nothing but a breath, more full of moisture than crying,
> a liquid, a sweat, an oil that has no name,
> a sharp motion,
> taking shape, making itself thick,
> the water is falling
> in slow drops
> toward the sea, toward its dry ocean,
> toward its wave without water.

Of course, the poem is not only about water. It is about the shapelessness of life itself, which tries to come together, to take on a body, but which can't always succeed, which ebbs into the uncooked, the ordinary, and the chaotic. The most extreme example of this occurs immediately following the passage above. Here, the poem falls back into a kind of desperate abundance, in which everything in sight, without plan or intention, is grasped and immediately released:

> I look at the wide summer, and a loud noise coming from a
> barn,
> wineshops, cicadas,
> towns, excitements,
> houses, girls
> sleeping with hands over their hearts,
> dreaming of pirates, of conflagrations,
> I look at ships,
> I look at trees of bone marrow
> bristling like mad cats,
> I look at blood, daggers and women's stockings,
> and men's hair,
> I look at beds, I look at corridors where a virgin is sobbing,
> I look at blankets and organs and hotels.

Neruda later mentions his "eyelid held open hideously," as if looking were a purely passive act and all this information were pouring in against his will. Actually, the looking changes direc tions so often that it is anything but passive. What is happening is that in going out toward the unknown, Neruda's senses are so widened that they take in many other possibilities as well as the central one. This is the essential factor of Neruda's voice, and is what makes him the opposite of a poet like Mallarmé. In most of Neruda's poems, there is a tremendous sense of impurity, of raw material as the poem emerges, a sense of abundance that continues as an undercurrent even in the more chiseled and formed poems. The result is poetry that forms itself out of unformed life, but always carries the great general power of that unformed life with it, as a kind of flood buoying up the words. At the end of "Sexual Water," the words have both the sting and separateness of form, and the energy, depth, and richness of chaos:

And even if I close my eyes and cover my heart over entirely,
I see the monotonous water falling
In big monotonous drops.
It is like a hurricane of gelatin,
like a waterfall of sperm and sea anemones.
I see a clouded rainbow hurrying.
I see its water moving over my bones.

Incidentally, this is not the way poetry is supposed to be written. The traditional view is that form and chaos are to be kept separate, and that art represents a triumph of the former over the latter. R. P. Blackmur says, "the chaos of private experience cannot be known or understood until it is projected and ordered in a form external to the consciousness that entertained it in a flux." How much more true this should be when it concerns the chaos of all experience, chaos itself, which is what Neruda is trying to deal with! But then again, how can chaos even become a subject of poetry if form is always fixed within an edge, always perfectly formed? Neruda's answer is to stretch form, to give it the kind of fluidity that will enable it to slip back into the raw and unformed now and then. After all, our sources are in the unformed—in the womb, in water. Naked poetry is an attempt to keep always in touch with those sources by centering itself in a continual act of emerging from them.

This act of emerging is like a snake sloughing off its skin. To slough off its skin means that a poem will exist in a particularly intimate relationship with its environment, since it has no skin, or rather, since its skin is opening up. This is what happens in the Neruda poem: it is open to the weather, the earth, the air, the sudden changes of the physical world. The poem is like a dance that regards its environment not as an illusionary or ideal space, but as a real place, with corners and edges that can be brought into the dance as raw material to be converted by expression—like a dance, in fact, in an actual environment, in a bedroom, a field, an office, a street. The poem isn't an object shaped from the outside; it is an act of emerging from these materials, from this environment, an environment that both pours into the poem and is sloughed off by it, as the poem sloughs off its skin. The poem is like a river that emerges from its materials and is impaled on them at the same time, a river that slides along its water, growing and changing with the forces, fissures, obstacles that the materials throw up in its path.

To slough off its skin also means that the poem in a sense has no past. The skin is the past of the poem as you read it. As you read a poem like Whitman's "There Was a Child Went Forth," the body of the poem passes through the words, and the words already read are the discarded skin. So the relationship of the words at the end of the poem to those at the beginning is not one that results from an accumulation of effects, as in Shakespeare's sonnets. Shakespeare uses a certain diction to unify a poem; words taken from the jargon of law or banking, for example, occur throughout a poem, giving it a kind of fullness. Shakespeare's sonnets close on themselves not only because of the closed form, but because of this use of diction; in fact, one follows upon the other. The poem becomes an act of filling itself. But naked poetry doesn't accumulate in this manner; it doesn't fill, it empties. It's like a river that never can store its energy, because that energy is always passing through it. It doesn't close, it opens. Actually, this is one polarity of naked poetry. Because naked poetry exists in a kind of open form, it will always have this tendency to unravel, to not accumulate. But many poets, when they feel the poem slipping through their fingers, feel the need to retain the poem somehow, to allow it to gather something at the same time that it empties itself. The most common device they resort to is repetition.

Why repetition? Repetition is the foundation of all form and rhythm. Even the devices of clothed poetry—rhyme, meter, and the patterns they exist in—are forms of repetition. Repetition, as Heidegger says about rhythm (in *On the Way to Language*), enables time to rest inside itself. If the temporal structures of our body—breathing, heartbeat, walking, etc.—didn't exist in the mode of repetition, then rest would be impossible for us. Repetition enables time to break, gather its energy, well up and break again. It gives time a tension-release structure with which it renews itself. It makes discontinuity possible in the midst of continuity, and we need discontinuity in order to gather ourselves and rest. The same is true about the cycles of repetition in the world around us—the repetition of night and day, the phases of the moon, the seasons. Naked poetry is usually submerged in process, in the processes of the body (breathing, heartbeat, walking), and in the processes of the world. Repetition is a kind of net in which to catch and hold these processes, while at the same time allowing them to exist as processes, that is, as movement. Repetition is movement that moves and stands still at the same time. Repetition gives the poem a past, but a past that is intimately related to the present. Whitman, who loved the present moment, also loved repetition as a way of preserving the present in the past:

> In vain the speeding or shyness,
> In vain the plutonic rocks send their old heat against my
>   approach,
> In vain the mastodon retreats beneath its own powder'd bones,
> In vain objects stand leagues off and assume manifold shapes,
> In vain the ocean settling in hollows and the great monsters
>   lying low,
> In vain the buzzard houses herself with the sky,
> In vain the snake slides through the creepers and logs,
> In vain the elk takes to the inner passes of the woods,
> In vain the razor-bill'd auk sails far north to Labrador,
> I follow quickly, I ascend to the nest in the fissure of the cliff.

There are other forms of repetition less radical than this, of course. Often, simply repeating the same word or sound three or four times in a poem has a similar effect. This effect is to give time and movement a kind of thickness. Whitman needed repetition in its strongest forms to check his forward momentum, which was always in danger of accelerating beyond his grasp. Repetition drags on time by giving it a resistance. This resistance is "in vain" in the Whitman passage; he still follows quickly, as he says at the end. But that very phrase, "in vain," strengthens the resistance enough to remind Whitman that it is a world of palpable things he's wading through, not just air.

If a naked poem is always sloughing off its skin, repetition is the new skin that grows to hold the poem in. Still, the most pure and also the most chancy kind of naked poetry is one that ignores repetition and allows itself simply not to accumulate. In its most radical form, each new word in the poem is a new discovery, a new testing of the unknown. Surrealism often does this. The danger is that no genuine discovery actually will take place; the poem becomes, as Wallace Stevens says, pure invention without discovery. There are some poems by Williams in which, rather than each new word, every two or three lines set off in a new direction. The poem becomes a series of slipknots coming undone. My favorite example is the well-known opening poem of *Spring and All:*

> By the road to the contagious hospital
> under the surge of the blue
> mottled clouds driven from the
> northeast—a cold wind. Beyond, the
> waste of broad, muddy fields
> brown with dried weeds, standing and fallen
>
> patches of standing water
> the scattering of tall trees
>
> All along the road the reddish
> purplish, forked, upstanding, twiggy
> stuff of bushes and small trees
> with dead, brown leaves under them
> leafless vines—

The movement of these lines is one of rapidly shifting, darting glances, some held, but most of them released the moment they occur. At this point, we are halfway through the poem and still haven't come to a completed sentence. The "cold wind" in the fourth line, for example, doesn't complete the sentence begun by the prepositions in the first two lines. The wind wasn't the thing described as by the road or under the surge of the clouds; rather, the wind enters as something that has unexpectedly asserted itself and interrupted the flow of the poem. Like Mallarmé, Williams often delays the subject and verb of a sentence to create suspense, but unlike Mallarmé, he also often simply withholds them completely. So we don't go back against the current of the language to plug in withheld information, as we do in Mallarmé. In Williams, we haven't the time to do this; the poem is shedding its skin too quickly. The opening sentence is incomplete because another sentence overlaps it; and this second sentence is also incomplete. This motion of overlapping incompletions is the dominant one in the poem. Each incomplete sentence outstrips the previous one, as if it began in the middle of it. The second stanza—"patches of standing water / the scattering of tall trees,"—consists of overlapping incomplete sentences that together overlap the incomplete sentence ending the first stanza. And so on, throughout the poem.

There are other motions in the midst of this dominant one. The five adjectives strung together in the third stanza have a descriptive quality, as adjectives do, but even more they have a gestural quality. While we are engaged in the act of reading them—"reddish / purplish, forked, upstanding, twiggy"—each one delays the expected noun that much more. They have both a rising and falling motion held simultaneously; falling, in that the sense of potential is rapidly diminished when we move from colors (reddish, purplish) to actual shapes (forked, etc.), and rising in that we feel each adjective will be the last, and give us the noun they all lead us to expect. There are many other

elements working here too: the staccato insistence of each isolated word, the hissing *sh* and *s* sounds intersected by upstanding *t*'s and *d*'s, both brought together, finally, in the noun,
"stuff," and the qualifications that follow it, "of bushes and
small trees." Here, the pace of the poem, the sense it has of
outstripping or shedding itself and barely keeping up with its
own shifts and discoveries, is increased by a sense of expectation in the words. The incompletions seem increasingly more
incomplete, until finally they break off altogether, and the first
sentence in the poem emerges:

> All along the road the reddish
> purplish, forked, upstanding, twiggy
> stuff of bushes and small trees
> with dead, brown leaves under them
> leafless vines—
>
> Lifeless in appearance, sluggish
> dazed spring approaches—

Matter-of-factly and simply, "dazed spring approaches"—the
first complete sentence in the poem. The line before it can be
read as either the spent last motion of all the previous overlapping phrases, or as something that modifies and introduces
"spring," or, most likely, as both. The verb, "approaches," has
done just that; the action it describes is not one that completes
itself, but one continually beginning, just as each overlapping
phrase in the poem is a new beginning, an attempt to keep up
or catch up with things.

The second half of the poem is not quite as breathless as the
first half, but does continue the same motion of overlapping
and outstripping, of passing through itself, as opposed to
gathering or accumulating.

> They enter the new world naked,
> cold, uncertain of all
> save that they enter. All about them
> the cold, familiar wind—

Now the grass, tomorrow
the stiff curl of wildcarrot leaf
One by one objects are defined—
It quickens: clarity, outline of leaf

But now the stark dignity of
entrance—Still, the profound change
has come upon them: rooted, they
grip down and begin to awaken

The hesitating motion—"Now," "But now," "Still,"—is the product of a lean language quick to react to the unexpected and the unpredictable. The entire poem is always and completely *in motion*, and the motion is continually unfinished—in fact, it's only begun—even with the last syllable. Many of Williams's poems are open-ended like this; they end at a pause, at the crest of a leap, at an open window or door. For example, the final lines of "St. Francis Einstein of the Daffodils":

The owner of the orchard
lies in bed
with open windows
and throws off his covers
one by one

This is what happens when a poem is an act, a temporal form. As Lawrence says, "no perfection, no consummation, nothing finished." The poem opens instead of closes. It is as if the poet were working his way through the space of the poem out into the space of the world. Whitman's poem, "When I Heard the Learn'd Astronomer," gives the same sense of things:

When I heard the learn'd astronomer,
When the proofs, the figures, were ranged in columns before
    me,
When I was shown the charts and diagrams, to add, divide, and
    measure them,
When I sitting heard the astronomer where he lectured with
    much applause in the lecture-room,

How soon unaccountable I became tired and sick,
Till rising and gliding out I wander'd off by myself,
In the mystical moist night-air, and from time to time,
Look'd up in perfect silence at the stars.

The poet going out into the world of things has to be ready for the shock of this silence. Language can only go so far (particularly language at that end of the spectrum that includes proofs, figures, charts, and diagrams). Whitman shows us, as Donne did in a different way, that great poets don't try to say everything; rather, they proceed through what can be said in order to bring us to the brink of what can't be said. There's not a particularly sophisticated or mellifluous use of words in this poem, and not a particularly brilliant or original idea expressed; in some respects, the idea flirts with sentimentality. But the poetry in a poem has little to do with ideas. This poem is one of Whitman's best, because of the deceptively artless simplicity of the words, because of the use of repetition coupled with periodic clauses to keep the words moving, and, most important, because of the sense of timing that tells it exactly when to stop. Although Whitman didn't always practice this kind of restraint, he always realized its importance. "I swear I see what is better than to tell the best," he said in "A Song of the Rolling Earth": "It is always to leave the best untold."

Whitman illustrates also one more point about naked poetry. In Mallarmé's poetry, we saw that the poem wants to be a thing but can't help but be an act—that is, the suppleness of the body undermines the thingness of the words. In naked poetry, the poem wants to be purely an act, wants to gesture *through* words rather than with them; yet, words in fact often crystallize and become things, and the poem often takes on the same kind of linguistic density that Mallarmé's poems possess. This simply means that there is no poetry that is pure, that can be exclusively in one tradition or the other. Speech always contains at least a residue of the opacity of language, and language always contains at least a residue of the bodily gestures of speech. We can never know, in fact, to what extent words alter the feeling and direction of any of Whitman's poems. Whitman gestures, but the gestures lodge in language, which *already* exists. The mark of a great poet may very well be the degree to which he can disguise the fact that already-existing words have dislodged his gesture from its intended curve. Interestingly enough, there is a kind of poetry being written today in which the poet no longer cares to disguise this fact; the dislodging of the gesture becomes part of the poem, part of the drama of the act of speech in the poem. I am thinking particularly of Robert Creeley; more on him shortly. First, to conclude this discussion of naked poetry, I want to look at a striking passage by Whitman in which the poem in fact does back up (in the sense of a river backing up) and crystallize in a word, and the word is not treated merely as a transparent gesture but as a thing in itself.

I am thinking of "Out of the Cradle Endlessly Rocking." To remind you of what the poem as a whole is like, and of Whitman's music at its best, I'll quote first the opening lines:

> Out of the cradle endlessly rocking,
> Out of the mocking-bird's throat, the musical shuttle,
> Out of the Ninth-month midnight,
> Over the sterile sands and the fields beyond, where the child
>   leaving his bed wander'd alone, bareheaded, barefoot,
> Down from the shower'd halo,
> Up from the patches of briers and blackberries,
> From the memories of the bird that chanted to me,
> From your memories sad brother, from the fitful risings and
>   fallings I heard,
> From under that yellow half-moon late-risen and swollen as if
>   with tears . . .

Here, the words are plastic, metamorphic. The center of the poem is not words, but a movement outward through words.

That is, rather than beginning in words, the poem begins in the intensity of felt life which breaks open like the boiling point of water and carries the words forward. But this movement forward is brought up short at the end of the poem and becomes blocked by a word, or rather, by a reality which, because it has to remain unopened, can only exist for us *as* a word:

> Whereto answering, the sea,
> Delaying not, hurrying not,
> Whisper'd me through the night, and very plainly before
>   daybreak,
> Lisp'd to me the low and delicious word death,
> And again death, death, death, death,
> Hissing melodious, neither like the bird nor like my arous'd
>   child's heart,
> But edging near as privately for me rustling at my feet,
> Creeping thence steadily up to my ears and laving me softly all
>   over,
> Death, death, death, death, death.

There's so much whispering and breathing outward in this passage that we can't help but remember that the word "death" rhymes with "breath," even if Whitman doesn't take advantage of the rhyme. In fact, he doesn't need to; the sensual fullness of "death" is enough for him. He's obviously in love with the word, and not ashamed to show it. The word has a magical power for him; he chants it, turns it this way and that, like an amulet, and *allows* the poem to pass almost entirely into the word. Of course, the word is a name, and perhaps one of the most unusual names in our language, since no one who uses or has ever used the language has experienced the reality the name calls forth. So it's a particularly impotent name, as names go, and few poets have ever said it as successfully as Whitman does here. Whitman, with the help of the ebbing rhythms of the ocean, wills the reality of death into the word. Or perhaps he seduces that reality, by singing to it. Whitman here is like Isis, who stung Re with a serpent and then withheld the cure for the sting until he told her his most secret name; when he did, he was completely in her power. Whitman in fact has seduced death into saying his own name.

Furthermore, Whitman has succeeded in uniting in this passage the opacity of language and the supple gestures of speech. He's also succeeded in uniting the sayable and the unsayable. These are perhaps the most brilliant features of this passage. The more you repeat a word, the more mute it becomes: you become aware of it not as a sound that denotes something, but simply as a kind of dumb sound. By chanting the word as he does, Whitman strikes an exact balance between on the one hand calling the reality of death forth with the insistence of his chant, the gesture of it, and on the other hand allowing that reality to pass over into silence, in the way any word repeated enough times passes over from meaning into pure, empty sound. All that can follow a passage like this is silence, itself a kind of death. Unfortunately, Whitman wrote another stanza after it. This has something of the effect of Beethoven continuing his A-minor quartet after the third movement, or of Rachmaninoff continuing his second symphony after his third movement. The only justification I can think of is that there's no way we can reenter the world with *that* kind of music in our heads; we need some ordinary language or ordinary music to ease the shock.

TWO The Cry of Its Occasion

THE PHRASE IS Stevens's—

> The poem is the cry of its occasion,
> Part of the res itself and not about it.
> ("An Ordinary Evening in New Haven")

but the burden of it lies with contemporary poetry, or at least
with certain contemporary poets, particularly those nourished
by the tradition of naked poetry. I take it to mean first of all that
the poem is not representational, the same way most modern
paintings are not representational. Robert Creeley insists that
poems are not picture postcards and that our attention should
be absorbed by an activity of words, just as in Jackson Pollock
our attention is absorbed by an activity of paint. When Creeley
says what is perhaps the most quoted dictum in contemporary
poetics—"form is never more than an extension of content"—
he is saying the same thing. Of course, even Creeley acknowledges (in *A Quick Graph*) that words drag things along with
them: "I think I first felt a poem to be what might exist in words
as primarily the fact of its own activity. Later, of course, I did

see that poems might comment on many things, and reveal
many attitudes and qualifications. Still, it was never what they
said *about* things that interested me."

I trace this sense of things back to Williams. In an early poem,
"The Wind Increases," he says:

> Good Christ what is
> a poet—if any
> > exists?
>
> a man
> whose words will
> > bite
> > > their way
>
> home—being actual
> having the form
> > of motion

"Being actual"—in other words, having their own weight, texture, autonomy. "Having the form of motion"—in other words,
embodying the gesture that gave rise to the words, the cry of
their occasion. Of course, a poem can be representational—as
most of Williams's are—*and* have the form of motion too. But
the representational quality will then be something transformed, embodied, an extension of the process of the poem, in
the same way the body and its clothing (and the things around
it) are transformed by the *act* of a dance. Again, as Williams
says in "The Desert Music": "NOT, prostrate, to copy nature /
but a dance!" And as he also says in one of his letters: "To copy
nature is a spineless activity; it gives us a sense of our mere
existence but hardly more than that. But to imitate nature involves the *verb:* we then ourselves *become* nature, and so invent
an object which is an extension of the process." At first glance,
the difference between "copy" and "imitate" doesn't appear to
be that significant. But the context—"we ourselves *become*
nature"—tells us that Williams's distinction is actually between

copying and embodying, between reporting about an already-existing world, and creating a world. From that it is only a short step to Creeley's sense of a poem being "the fact of its own activity," not even necessarily natural, or linked with natural processes, but rather original and unique in itself.

I suspect that this is the most naked poetry that we have, that it shows by its example the nakedness of all great poetry, of even a sonnet by Donne. The words in a poem by Williams are entirely transparent gestures of his body—they have *that* form of motion, the quickness and shifting pace of the body and mind dancing together—and they are at the same time opaque, in the sense that they refer to their own activity before they ever refer to an "external" world. Actually, that external world *is* made present in a poem by Williams, but not by being referred to. The poem is not "about" the world; rather, the world is itself drawn into the dance of the words and recreated and refreshed there. In Williams, the world is freshened by speech, by its transformation into speech. There is nothing more clear and at the same time more self-delighting than this kind of poetry, which by drawing things into words liberates them. The world in Williams's poems is a wave that passes up through the body of the poet into words in one uninterrupted flow; and the flow is the poem.

I mention all this by way of introduction to Creeley. In both poets, the world is not so much represented by the content of a poem as enacted by its gestures. In Creeley, those gestures are hesitant and tenuous, and so the world is hesitant and tenuous as well. When Creeley says,

> Pain is a flower like that one,
> like this one,
> like that one,
> like this one

we are aware not so much of the simile as of the repetition of

pronouns, perhaps the least resonant words a poet could choose
to repeat. We are also aware of a motion, an action; the speaker
is designating, pointing, and discarding as he points, in the
same way people pull petals off flowers. So we are aware of the
language as an activity and, by extension, of the words as
words; rather than the words serving to refer us to flowers, the
simile of the flowers points to the words that embody it. In fact,
the pronouns "this one" and "that one" probably refer to nothing other than themselves. The pain described, as in many of
Creeley's poems, is the painful process of language itself, of
speaking. If "form is never more than an extension of content,"
that is because, every poem being an utterance, its subject will
invariably be its own act. Williams's subject is usually the
simultaneous penetration of the act of the poem and the activity
of the natural world. In Creeley, that natural world has only the
most provisional existence; is exists mostly as a pronoun, as
"you," "that," or "it." Without that weight, his poems seem
often about to disappear into the air as quickly as a gesture
does. Either that, or else they barely catch up with the world,
barely attain it.

In the midst of this activity, the dominant fact is the poet's
body. The world makes itself felt on one side of speech as the
pull of the Other, and on the other side of speech as the distur-
bance, need, dislocation of the body. In Creeley, the body is the
"field" his friend Charles Olson talked about, the openness a
poet composes in. However, the body is also closed, and often
deflects the intended gesture of the poem. Actually, Creeley's
poems are seldom intended; they are rather found, attained, or
as he says, permitted. For Creeley, the poem is an act of speech
that struggles against the intransigence of language as a form of
the body. Or rather, language has two forms: the act that gives
birth to it (speech) and the form that closes around that act and

makes it an object, the form of given words and structures that constitute our cultural body (language). The result is, usually, pain: the sense that no word is ever quite the right one, every word in a sense a lie, or at best a compromise, and words in combination a conspiracy:

> As soon as
> I speak, I
> speaks. It
>
> wants to
> be free but
> impassive lies
>
> in the direction
> of its
> words.

The "it" in Creeley is usually the widest possible "it"—in this case, an impulse that gives rise to speech, but also the world that needs to be spoken, that wells up within the body of the poet and wants to be free. However, it lies impassive because the words it gestures weigh down on the gesture and limit it, or at least deflect it. The poem, as all of Creeley's do, *enacts* this weight and deflection: the hesitations, the broken, discontinuous quality, the frantic enjambments and short lines that carry the energy of the poem in jagged spurts, like someone continually catching his breath—all of these are not only expressions of, but also the fact of the act of speech struggling upstream against the language it is wading in.

Of course, this sense of the difficulties of speech drives the poems themselves that much more completely into the mouth, into the unmediated act of speech. We are most conscious of our bodies when they push against an unmoveable or barely moveable thing. In Creeley, we are conscious of speech *as* speech always because of this pushing against language:

> He pushes behind the words
> which, awkward, catch
> and turn him to a disturbed
> and fumbling man.

This struggle also results in a poetry of discovery, discovery never planned, but always happened upon, seemingly by accident. In the prose section of *A Day Book,* he says, "Whether errors, as meaning to write *Echoes* becomes *Whether,* as the finger meant to strike the E key, hits the W—and the thought moves to include it, to use it in the thought, and so on." In other words, meaning becomes almost an accident of the act of language in Creeley. He tries on and discards words as if none of them exactly fit, so that what is important is not the accomplished word, but this act of thinking, of testing and searching. This is why his poems are so provisional, and their relationship to existence so risky. They could easily pass out of existence themselves, without leaving a trace—or, unexpectedly, existence could suddenly pass into and occupy them. They avoid things so assiduously that it is often a shock to see a thing suddenly and spontaneously born within one of them:

> As I sd to my
> friend, because I am
> always talking—John, I
>
> sd, which was not his
> name, the darkness sur-
> rounds us, what
>
> can we do against
> it, or else, shall we &
> why not, buy a goddam big car,
>
> drive, he sd, for
> Christ's sake, look
> our where yr going.

Which was not his name—then we are not in "reality," but rather in an activity of words ("because I am always talking"). But this activity of words, however provisional, *is* a reality. In fact, it gives birth, out of its act of speculation—why not buy a car—to a literal car: "drive, he sd." Creeley himself (in *A Quick Graph*) has described this activity as akin to driving. The road, he says, literally creates itself in front of you, so it is crucial to pay *attention*, attention "to what is happening in the writing (the road) one is, in the sense suggested, following."

This attention is often excruciating, and it costs Creeley a tremendous effort of the will. His poems are incredibly *tiring*. Actually, "will" is the wrong word. The poet's job is to *follow* the road creating itself in front of him. This takes extreme caution, care, accuracy; it also takes an equally extreme sense of the possible. I know of no other poet in whom care and the sense of possibility are so strongly united. Each line is a new attempt to fix something, and yet each line is both brittle and temporary, conscious of being finite. Each line, in fact, could end at any moment, even before the first word is over. Creeley has made the *line* in poetry a fearful thing, a gesture whose curve is always tentative. Often, the line breaks at the verbs, and often the verbs are copulas. So the gesture, the act of the poem, is one that acknowledges continually junctures in the world, gaps, holes, cracks. Consider this poem, "The Turn":

> Each way the turn
> twists, to be apprehended:
> now she is
> there, now she
>
> is not, goes, but
> did she, having gone,
> went before
> the eye saw
>
> nothing. The tree
> cannot walk, all its
> going must
> be violence. They listen

> to the saw cut, the
> roots scream. And in eating
> even a stalk of celery
> there will be pathetic screaming.
>
> But what we want
> is not what we get.
> What we saw, we think
> we will see again?
>
> We will not. Moving,
> we will
> move, and then
> stop.

I am conscious, in this poem, of a movement continually hesitating, being interrupted, breaking off—of each line as a cliff and each sentence with a chasm between it and the next one. This sense of great gaps in the poem, of things left out, the *absence* of things, exists despite the equally strong sense of compression, of the contents existing under enormous pressure. Nothing is ever *held* in this poem. Each sentence makes a new beginning. I am conscious of a world of discrete things, pieces, fragments, and of a movement going through the pieces and trying to string them together. This sense of discreteness is equally one of words and of those things the words enact:

> now she is
> there, now she
>
> is not, goes. . . .

The copula tries to hold together what can't be held, what divides against itself continually. When the poem manages to describe, it describes pieces: a tree cut up, celery eaten. The chief action is one of cutting, so that even to see—"what we saw"—is not to create a link, but to sever one. Only the *rhythm* of these junctures holds out the possibility of movement. This is actually one of the most profound definitions of movement I know of, possibly because it acknowledges so beautifully the bodily act of language as well as, say, the literal act of walking: movement is a rhythm of absences. Or perhaps movement is the discovery of a rhythm of absences, discovery in the sense that the rhythm actually grows out of stumbling, breaking off, hesitating:

> What we saw, we think
> we will see again?
>
> We will not. Moving,
> we will
> move, and then
> stop.

Movement—surely by extension, any movement, psychic, emotional, liguistic, bodily—movement is equally painful and necessary. Could someone unfamiliar with the details of Creeley's life know that this is the poem of a one-eyed man? Probably not. But knowing that, how can we fail to sense that two-dimensional space, that sudden foreshortening, and that care and stumbling that has to *make* itself confident through an extreme self-consciousness coupled with the necessity to take chances, to be *in* the act, not ahead of or behind it? These are psychic, emotional, linguistic qualities, but they have the body as their ground and are all drawn together by the one bodily gesture that is the poem.

Creeley has been called a minimalist, I suppose because of the strong sense of absence in his poems, of what he leaves out. However, unlike minimalist painters and sculptors, Creeley allows the poem always to embody the act that gives birth to it, with all its slips, hesitations, failures, and discoveries. In this sense, he reminds me more of the sculptor Giacometti than of any of the minimalists. Sartre's comments on Giacometti could apply equally to Creeley. Space, Sartre says, is a terror for Giacometti. Space is not generosity, but superfluity; it dwarfs things. "For him, to sculpture is to trim the fat from space, to compress it and wring from it all its exteriority." Furthermore, Giacometti's figures are always ten steps (or twenty steps, or whatever) away, no matter how close the viewer gets to them. Giacometti places distance within our reach. I sense the same thing in Creeley. He dwarfs our own language and shows us our distance from it, as if it were a foreign language we only half know, dimly recognizable. Actually, he shows us simultaneously our intimacy with and our distance from language. In Creeley, language in the form of speech is our very consciousness and body, the *act* of these, and yet in the form of an object, of preexisting words, it is something divided from us, at a distance.

Like Giacometti with his sculptures, Creeley stretches his poems to the breaking point of language. Failure is always built into that kind of gesture. Either the language in fact does break, or, if it doesn't, the poet thinks he could have stretched it further. This kind of poem contains its own dream of perfection, as Giacometti's sculptures do. As Sartre puts it, "almost as soon as they are produced he goes on to dream of women that are thinner, taller, lighter, and it is through his work that he envisions the ideal by virtue of which he judges it imperfect." In fact, this is similar to a sense of things Creeley describes:

> I know two women
>   and the one
> is tangible substance
>   flesh and bone.
>
> The other in my mind
>   occurs.
> She keeps her strict
>   proportion there.

It is fascinating to me that these two men whose relationship to their respective materials is so similar should also take women as their chief subject. However naked their own gestures are, they are also trimmed of superfluity by a strong sense of the Other. The sense of the incomplete in their work may well be that bodily need for the Other that passes into their very materials.

In Creeley, that need is inseparable from the sheer immediacy of the act of his poems. "Speech / is a mouth" because words are "full / of holes / aching." And words are full of holes because the act of speech grows out of love, and love out of need:

> Locate *I*
> *love you* some-
> where in
>
> teeth and
> eyes, bite
> it but
>
> take care not
> to hurt, you
> want so
>
> much so
> little. Words
> say everything,
>
> *I*
> *love you*
> again,
>
> then what
> is emptiness
> for. To
>
> fill, fill.
> I heard words
> and words full
>
> of holes
> aching. Speech
> is a mouth.

The primary interest in this poem may very well be "the fact of its own activity"—after all, it is about language. But this activity is not so narrow as to exclude the body and the world. It's no accident that Creeley's "example" of language is "*I love you,*" a phrase that resonates throughout the poem and opens the words in the mode of desire. Rather than *referring* us to desire and to its object, the act of the poem *is* that desire. This desire carries the body and the Other along with itself, as its two outer limits. The physical world is not described, but is briefly opened with the gesture of the poem. The poem cuts a furrow in the world by drawing that world into its words—not referential words, like windows, but words charged with need, mouths. All the ingredients of pictorial poetry are here: a common world, two people, love. But none of these ingredients is pictorial; rather, they are all actual, in the sense of things enacted. We are conscious of a voice speaking now, this moment. We are not conscious of language as a virtual space, related to the actual world as radar is to the sky, but of language, simply, as an act that struggles against itself. At the center of that struggle there is a mouth, and, flowing into it and disappearing into its activity, a body on one side, and a world on the other.

Afterword

Afterword

I HAVE ENDED this book by looking at a poet for whom words are almost purely gestures not in order to point out a "new" kind of poetry, but to make clear the perspective from which the entire book is written. The poems of Donne, Blake, and Mallarmé are equally embodiments, enactments; words gesture and dance in them every bit as much as they do in Creeley. The only difference between the work of the others and that of Creeley is that in Creeley the gesture is more apparent because the language is more opaque, that is, nonrepresentational. It is as if a river had suddenly become a rapids, so that we are more aware of it as movement than as water.

It strikes me that there is a theory of the poetic impulse, and perhaps an aesthetics, implied by this view. Of course, there is the central theory, that poetry is an act of the body, and so an embodiment. Beyond this—or before it—I have the sense that a poem always arises out of desire, and that the best poems are those in which the desire passes into the language. This is especially true of Donne and Blake. In Creeley, desire always faces immediate and apparent obstacles; we are negotiating rapids. In Whitman, desire is generalized and spread out, as if on an ocean, so that at times it almost seems not to exist. Then, however, we are taken up by a swell that gathers from across the whole surface of the poem, and we find it impossible to say when that swell was never actually present.

In Mallarmé, there are no swells, and no rapids. Impotence, the lack of desire, is his central theme. But this lack enters the words in such a way as to mock them and mock their attempts to exclude all other words, to exclude the world and shine alone. What else is a lack but a form of desire, or at least its first condition? The more self-sufficient Mallarmé's words become, the more the silence around them takes on the form of a gap to be bridged, a distance to be traversed, a need. By excluding desire, Mallarmé's language calls desire up that much more into the interstices between words; desire becomes the very net in which the poem is held, the space it occupies. Mallarmé demonstrates the curse of the impotent, for whom desire is never present and yet never absent.

Mallarmé probably knew that failure is built into the very structure of desire. Either it can never be fulfilled, or when it is fulfilled it dies, and a new desire starts up immediately. In many respects, Creeley and Mallarmé are similar poets, especially in the tortured syntax of their poems and the linguistic density and opacity of their language. But the chief difference between them is that one rejects failure and one accepts it. Creeley's desire that always meets obstacles is equally a recognition of the fact that failure and compromise are built into the structure of language. Mallarmé undoubtedly knew that by rejecting imperfection and failure, his poems would be continually haunted by it, like Hérodiade, who loves being a virgin because she wants to live in the terror her hair causes her. Actually, "Hérodiade" (along with "L'Après-Midi d'un Faune"), is one of the few poems of Mallarmé that expresses desire; but paradoxically, the desire it expresses is a desire not to have desire, not to be imperfected by desire. The quality of density in Mallarmé's language, then, is perhaps a desire turned back on itself, always threatening to strangle or devour itself.

So even in Mallarmé, desire is a crucial—perhaps *the* crucial—factor in the language. If I had to construct an aesthetics, then, it would go like this: when speech enters poetry, it becomes an erotic activity. Or, to say the same thing, it becomes poetic because it *feels* erotic. Need or desire passes into words, so that they become thicker, take on volume and weight, and yet become open, incomplete. My own language here is so obviously sexual in its references as to seem reductionist. But in fact, as Maurice Merleau-Ponty puts it, everything is sexual in nature, even if there is nothing that is purely sexual (including sex itself).

When I say that speech, entering poetry, becomes erotic, I mean that its sexual nature is heightened. Words which by themselves are asleep, together are awakened by desire. Of course, the desire may be sublimated, as in a dance. But what do we mean by sublimation except to say that desire is given a curve, a motion, a volume and activity, when it passes through the body?

To say that desire passes through the body assumes that there is something outside the body which attracts and draws it out. I think this is true. An aesthetics of desire requires a sense of the Other. The Other may be a thing, a creature, a place, a person—the occasion of the poem as a mode of address—or it may be the audience or a virtual audience. The strength of sound and meaning in a poem comes from this sense of the Other, because speech is pulled taut by reciprocity. The poet speaks and listens at the same time. To listen means to allow: one allows language to accumulate the possibility of a presence.

This is how Being enters a poem and touches it; Being is allowed—which shows the intimate relationship to language it has, since Being is also aloud. In other words, the representative of the Other on the poet's body is his ear. When poets talk about writing with the ear (as Creeley often does), they are talking about this virtual presence of the Other, which demands that language be *heard*. Poets for whom improvisation is important need especially to have this sense of the Other. Without it, the language goes slack, the ear closes up, and the poem becomes chatter, wallowing around in words, self-indulgence. The poet then closes off his most crucial instinct: a sense of the unexpected.

The poets I've looked at in this book all have a strong sense of the Other, even Mallarmé, whose poem is in fact in the second person, as Donne's and Blake's are. A poem is first of all an activity. Desire enters the words, wakes them up, they stir, become animated; the Other gives this animation a vector, a direction. The Other always tugs at the poem, like a siren. Speech in the best poems, caught in the tug and pull between Self and Other, body and world, is continually in motion. Speech is a mouth, and the body is carried up into its activity— just as the entire body, not just the mouth, is present when we bite an apple—carried up into and *through* it instead of simply being a sack hanging down from the mouth, a thing in itself.

I should add that for the poet a truly erotic language is one in which pleasure is not only taken but given. The poet is always in love with the sound of his own voice, as a baby is; but if that's all he is in love with, then he's in trouble.

Of course, this is only an aesthetics and must yield in the end to the pressure of the moment and the sudden presence of the unexpected.

Bibliography

Bachelard, Gaston. *The Poetics of Reverie*, trans. Daniel Russell. New York: Orion Press, 1969.

Barnstone, Willis, ed. *Modern European Poetry*. New York: Bantam Books, 1966.

Barthes, Roland. *The Pleasure of the Text*, trans. Richard Miller. New York: Hill and Wang, 1975.

———. *Writing Degree Zero*, trans. Annette Lavers and Colin Smith. New York: Hill and Wang, 1968.

Beckett, Samuel. *Watt*. New York: Grove, 1959.

Berry, Francis. *Poetry and the Physical Voice* New York: Oxford University Press, 1962.

Blackmur, R. P. *Language as Gesture: Essays in Poetry*. New York: Harcourt, Brace, 1954.

Blake, William. *Complete Writings*, ed. Geoffrey Keynes. London: Oxford University Press, 1966.

Bly, Robert, ed. and trans. *Lorca and Jimenez: Selected Poems*. Boston: Beacon Press, 1973.

———. *Neruda and Vallejo: Selected Poems*, trans. Robert Bly, John Knoepfle, and James Wright. Boston: Beacon Press, 1971.

Brown, Norman O. *Love's Body*. New York: Random House, 1966.

Burnshaw, Stanley. *The Seamless Web*. New York: Braziller, 1970.

Burroughs, William S. *Nova Express*. New York: Grove, 1964.

Cassirer, Ernst. *The Philosophy of Symbolic Forms*, trans. Ralph Manheim. 3 vols. New Haven: Yale University Press, 1953.

Chomsky, Noam. *Chomsky: Selected Readings*, ed. J. P. B. Allen and Paul Van Buren. New York: Oxford University Press, 1971.

Collingwood, R. G. *The Principles of Art*. New York: Oxford University Press, 1958.

Creeley, Robert. *A Day Book*. New York: Scribner, 1972.

———. *A Quick Graph; Collected Notes and Essays*, ed. Donald Allen. San Francisco: Four Seasons Foundation, 1976.

———. *For Love: Poems, 1950–1960*. New York: Scribner, 1962.

———. *Pieces*. New York: Scribner, 1969.

———. *Words*. New York: Scribner, 1967.

Derrida, Jacques. *La Dissémination*. Paris: Éditions de Seuil, 1972.

———. *Of Grammatology*, trans. Gayatri Chakravorty. Baltimore: Johns Hopkins University Press, 1976.

———. "Structure, Sign, and Play in the Discourse of the Human Sciences," in *The Structuralist Controversy: The Languages of Criticism and the Sciences of Man*. Baltimore: Johns Hopkins Press, 1970.

Donne, John. *The Complete Poetry of John Donne*, ed. John T. Shawcross. New York: New York University Press, 1968.

Driver, Tom F. "Beckett by the Madeleine," *Columbia University Forum* (Summer, 1961), pp. 21–25.

Eliot, T. S. *The Complete Poems and Plays 1909–1950*. New York: Harcourt, Brace and World, 1952.

Empson, William. *Seven Types of Ambiguity*. London: Chatto and Windus, 1953.

Foucault, Michel. *The Archeology of Knowledge*, trans. A. M. Sheridan Smith. New York: Pantheon, 1972.

———. *The Order of Things: An Archeology of the Human Sciences*. New York: Pantheon, 1970.

Fowlie, Wallace. *Mallarmé*. Chicago: University of Chicago Press, 1970.

Hartman, Geoffrey. *The Unmediated Vision: An Interpretation of Wordsworth, Hopkins, Rilke, and Valéry*. New Haven: Yale University Press, 1954.

Heidegger, Martin. *On the Way to Language*, trans. Peter D. Hertz. New York: Harper and Row, 1971.

———. *Poetry, Language, Thought*, trans. Albert Hofstadter. New York: Harper and Row, 1971.

Herbert, George. *The Works of George Herbert*, ed. F. E. Hutchinson. Oxford: Clarendon Press, 1941.

Herrick, Robert. *Poems.* New York: E. P. Dutton, 1936.

Hugo, Richard. "Letters to Friends: 19 Poems," *American Poetry Review* (January/February, 1973), pp. 25–32.

Kenner, Hugh. *The Pound Era.* Berkeley: University of California Press, 1971.

Lawrence, David Herbert. *Lady Chatterley's Lover.* New York: Grove, 1959.

———. "Poetry of the Present," in *The Complete Poems of D. H. Lawrence,* ed. Vivian de Sola Pinto and F. Warren Roberts. New York: Viking, 1971.

Lorca, Federico Garcia. *The Selected Poems of Federico Garcia Lorca,* ed. Francisco Garcia Lorca and Donald M. Allen. New York: New Directions, 1961.

Mallarmé, Stephane. *Mallarmé,* ed. Anthony Hartley. Harmondsworth, England: Penguin Books, 1965.

Merleau-Ponty, Maurice. *Phenomenology of Perception,* trans. Colin Smith. London: Routledge and Kegan Paul, 1962.

Nelson, Cary. *The Incarnate Word: Literature as Verbal Space.* Urbana: University of Illinois Press, 1973.

Rilke, Rainer Maria. *Duino Elegies and the Sonnets to Orpheus,* trans. A. Poulin, Jr. Boston: Houghton Mifflin, 1977.

———. *Selected Works,* vol. 1: *Prose,* trans. G. C. Houston. New York: New Directions, 1961.

Rimbaud, Jean-Nicolas-Arthur. *Complete Works, Selected Letters,* trans. Wallace Fowlie. Chicago: University of Chicago Press, 1966.

Roethke, Theodore. *Collected Poems.* New York: Doubleday, 1966.

Sartre, Jean-Paul. *Essays in Aesthetics,* trans. Wade Baskin. New York: Philosophical Library, 1963.

Saussure, Ferdinand de. *Course in General Linguistics,* ed. Charles Bally and Albert Sechehaye, trans. Wade Baskin. New York: Philosophical Library, 1959.

Shakespeare, William. *The Poems,* ed. J. C. Maxwell. Cambridge: Cambridge University Press, 1969.

Simic, Charles. *What the Grass Says.* Santa Cruz, California: Kayak Books, n.d.

Stendhal. *The Red and the Black,* trans. Lloyd C. Parks. New York: New American Library, 1970.

Stevens, Wallace. *Collected Poems.* New York: Alfred A. Knopf, 1967.

———. *Opus Posthumus: Poems, Plays, Prose,* ed. Samuel French Morse. New York: Knopf, 1957.

Valéry, Paul. *The Art of Poetry* (vol. 7 of *The Collected Works of Paul Valéry*, ed. Jackson Mathews), trans. Denise Folliot. New York: Pantheon, 1958.

Wakoski, Diane. "The Craft of Plumbers, Carpenters, and Mechanics," *American Poetry Review* (January/February, 1973), pp. 46–47.

Wellek, René, and Austin Warren. *Theory of Literature*. New York: Harcourt, Brace, 1949.

Whitman, Walt. *Leaves of Grass and Selected Prose*, ed. John A. Kouwenhoven. New York: Random House, 1950.

Williams, William Carlos. *Collected Earlier Poems*. New York: New Directions, 1963.

———. *Collected Later Poems*. New York: New Directions, 1963.

———. *Paterson*. New York: New Directions, 1963.

———. *Pictures from Brueghel, and Other Poems*. New York: New Directions, 1962.

———. *Selected Letters*, ed. John C. Thirwall, New York: Ivan Obolensky, 1957.

Wittgenstein, Ludwig. *Philosophical Investigations*, trans. G. E. M. Anscombe. Oxford: B. Blackwell, 1963.

Wordsworth, William. *Poetry and Prose*, selected by W. M. Merchant. Cambridge: Harvard University Press, 1967.

Yeats, W. B. *Collected Poems*. New York: Macmillan, 1956.

Index